SPECIAL SERIES No. 29   FEBRUARY 1945

JAPANESE DEFENSE
AGAINST
AMPHIBIOUS OPERATIONS

MILITARY INTELLIGENCE DIVISION
WAR DEPARTMENT • WASHINGTON, D. C.

Published by Books Express Publishing
Copyright © Books Express, 2011
ISBN 978-1-780390-79-6

Books Express publications are available from all good retail and online booksellers. For publishing proposals and direct ordering please contact us at: info@books-express.com

CONFIDENTIAL

SPECIAL SERIES NO. 29　　　　　　　　FEBRUARY 1945

JAPANESE DEFENSE

AGAINST

AMPHIBIOUS OPERATIONS

MILITARY INTELLIGENCE DIVISION

WAR DEPARTMENT　•　WASHINGTON, D. C.

CONFIDENTIAL

MILITARY INTELLIGENCE
SERVICE
WAR DEPARTMENT
WASHINGTON 25, D. C., February 1945

SPECIAL SERIES
NO. 29
MIS 461

Notice

1. SPECIAL SERIES is published for the purpose of providing officers with reasonably confirmed information from official and other reliable sources.
2. Reproduction within the military service is encouraged provided that (1) the source is stated, (2) the classification is maintained, and (3) one copy of the publication in which the material is reproduced is forwarded to the Military Intelligence Service, War Department, Washington 25, D. C.

DISTRIBUTION:

AAF (10); AGF (56); ASF (2); T of Opn (IB, C, SWPA, POA) (200), (MTO, ETO) (5); Dept (2); Arm & Sv Bd (2); Def Comd (5); Tech Sv (2); SvC (2); PC&S, ZI (1); USMA (5); A (10); CHQ (10); D 7 (20); T/O & E (to units in POA, CBI, SWPA, & ZI only) 3–217 (1); 5–411 (3); 5–415 (2); 5–417 (1); 5–510–1S (5); 5–511S (3); 5–515S (2); 5–525S (2); 5–535S (2); 5–555S (2); 5–557S (2); 7–16 (5); 7–17 (3); 8–15 (1); 8–65 (1); 8–187 (1); 8–661 (1); 8–667 (1); 9–7 (1); 9–17 (1); 10–57 (1); 10–67 (1); 10–197 (1); 11–147S (1); 17–115 (2); 17–117 (1); 17–125 (2); 17–127 (1); 19–37 (1); 19–57 (1); 55–37 (1).

For explanation of symbols, see FM 21–6.

CONFIDENTIAL

Contents

	Page
CHAPTER I. TACTICS AND ORGANIZATION	1
Tactics	1
Doctrine	1
Basic Principles	4
Defense of Attu	7
Use of Terrain—Biak	8
Kiska	15
Tarawa Atoll	15
Kwajalein	19
Munda and Vila	21
Eniwetok	23
Makin	23
Saipan	27
General Estimate	28
Organization	30
CHAPTER II. BEACH OBSTACLES, BARRICADES, AND MINES	33
Introduction	33
Barbed Wire	36
Concrete Obstacles and Log Barricades	37
Improvised Obstacles	39
Tank Barriers and Traps	40
Mines	41
CHAPTER III. FORTIFICATIONS AND AIRFIELDS	44
Concrete Installations	44
Construction Methods	44
Blockhouses	46
Pillboxes	48
Casements	50
Shelters	50
Concrete-covered Steel	52
Prefabricated Concrete	54
Non-Concrete Installations	54
Shelters	54
Bunkers	54
Pillboxes	55
Camouflage and Dummy Positions	57
Airfields	63
General Description	63
Typical Fields	64

	Page
CHAPTER IV. JAPANESE COAST DEFENSE GUNS	66
8-Inch Guns	66
6-Inch Guns	69
14-cm and 12-cm Guns	73
4.7-Inch Guns	77
8-cm and 75-mm Guns	79
Heavy Guns Not Yet Encountered	81
Field Artillery in Coast Defense	86
Guns Captured by the Japanese	87
CHAPTER V. DUAL-PURPOSE, ANTIAIRCRAFT, AND MACHINE GUNS	93
Dual-Purpose and Antiaircraft Guns	93
Mobile Guns	103
Fixed Guns	105
Machine Guns	110
Heavy Machine Guns	110
Light Machine Guns	111
CHAPTER VI. DETECTION AND COMMUNICATION	113
Radar	113
Description of Early Warning Equipment	113
Searchlight Control	116
Radio	117
Searchlights	119

Illustrations

Figure	Page
1. Japanese coast defense gun on Saipan	3
2. Cave used by Japanese in defense of Biak	9
3. Japanese observation post on Biak	10
4. Coast defense gun emplacements on Guam	11
5. Map of Guam showing landing beaches	12
6. Cave defenses on Guam	13
7. Map of Japanese defenses on North Head, Kiska	14
8. Map of Japanese defense installations on Betio	16
9. Typical shore line defenses along southwest shore of Betio	17
10. Portion of sea wall on Betio (above); Japanese barricade positions behind sea wall (below)	18
11. Concrete and log defenses on Betio	19
12. Aerial photograph of Namur Island	20
13. Coral stone fortifications, Kwajalein	21
14. Map of defenses of Engebi Island, Eniwetok	22
15. Japanese pillbox on shore line at Munda	23
16. Japanese pillboxes on Kwajalein beach	24
17. Japanese light tank dug in for defense of Eniwetok	25
18. Japanese 4.7-inch gun emplacement on Eniwetok	25
19. Map of defenses of Saipan	26
20. Camouflaged Japanese field piece captured intact on Saipan	27
21. Japanese 6-inch gun emplacement on Tinian	28
22. Barbed wire beach obstacles on Guam	36
23. Looking seaward through barbed wire entanglemments on Betio beach	37
24. Coral and log obstacles on Guam	38
25. Wire and log obstacle on Guam	39
26. Tank trap just off a Betio beach	41
27. Rear view (above) and inside wall of heavily constructed concrete pillbox (below)	45
28. (a) Rear view of heavy circular concrete pillbox on Roi. (b) Closeup of the circular pillbox shows the steel embrasure lining and cover	47
29. Camouflaged wall with rifle embrasures	48
30. Wrecked reinforced concrete emplacement for 6-inch gun on Saipan	49
31. Views of "Air Defense Command Post" on Betio	51
32. Exterior and interior views of Japanese steel pillbox encountered on Betio	53
33. Log pillbox, Buna	55
34. Gunport in Japanese log and sand pillbox on Betio	56
35. Camouflaged gun position (Gilbert Islands)	58
36. Camouflaged 8-inch battery on Betio	59
37. Japanese 3-inch gun well camouflaged on a Saipan beach	59
38. Dummy range finder on Saipan	61
39. Dummy antiaircraft gun	62
40. Dummy coast defense gun	62
41. Left side of 8-inch gun emplacement on Betio	66

Figure	Page
42. 8-inch gun emplacement on southwest point of Betio island	67
43. Looking from lower to upper piece of 8-inch gun tandem emplacement on Betio	68
44. Views of 8-inch short naval gun	70
45. Views of 6-inch 40 caliber coast defense gun with shield	71
46. Armstrong-Whitworth Model 1900 6-inch naval gun	72
47. A Japanese 6-inch gun emplaced on Chonito Cliff, Guam	72
48. Two views of 1912 Model 15-cm gun	73
49. Views of 14-cm naval gun emplaced in turret on Betio	74
50. Japanese 14-cm naval gun with battleship casemate type of shield at Enogai Inlet, New Georgia (above); rear view of 14-cm naval gun (below)	75
51. 14-cm naval gun at Enogai Inlet, New Georgia, in open emplacement	76
52. (a) 12-cm (120-mm) Model 3 naval gun; (b) Another view of the 120-mm Model 3 naval gun	78
53. Views of Model 3 (1914) 12-cm naval gun with destroyer type of shield	80
54. 24-cm gun (above); 28-cm howitzer (below)	82
55. 6-inch 40 caliber coast defense gun encountered on Guam	83
56. 24-cm gun, Schneider, railway mount	85
57. Two types of emplacements for the Model 10 (1921) 120-mm dual-purpose gun	94
58. Model 10 (1921) 120 mm dual-purpose gun	95
59. Installing one gun of a twin-mount 127-mm Model 89 gun	96
60. Model 88 (1928) 75-mm dual-purpose gun	97
61. Model 10 (1921) 3-inch (76.2-mm) naval dual-purpose gun in banked emplacement	98
62. Model 10 (1921) 3-inch (76.2-mm) naval dual-purpose gun captured on Guadalcanal	98
63. Vickers type, 40-mm machine cannon, single mount	99
64. Vickers type, 40-mm machine cannon, twin mount	100
65. Model 98 (1938) 20-mm machine cannon	101
66. Views of 25-mm naval automatic cannon, twin mount	102
67. 25-mm automatic cannon, triple mount	103
68. 105-mm army type mobile antiaircraft gun	104
69. 105-mm antiaircraft gun with crew	104
70. Model 89 (1929) 127-mm twin-mount naval dual-purpose gun	105
71. Views of Model 89 (1929) twin-mount naval dual-purpose gun	106
72. Twin-mount Model 89 (1929) naval dual-purpose gun	107
73. Twin-mount 127-mm naval dual-purpose gun positions on Betio	108
74. Diagram of 3-gun dual-purpose battery on Wake Island	109
75. Japanese 75-mm antiaircraft gun on Guam	109
76. Japanese radar screen	115
77. Japanese mobile searchlight	120
78. Japanese searchlight on Betio	120
79. Searchlight captured near Munda airfield	121
80. Searchlight and sound detector	122

CHAPTER I.

Tactics and Organization

Tactics

Doctrine

Japanese basic tactical doctrine is characterized by a strong aversion to the defensive. Defensive operations are considered merely a temporary phase of combat necessitated by the momentary preponderance of the strength of hostile forces. The Japanese try to terminate this phase as quickly as possible by whittling down the superiority of the enemy until they can revert to the offensive and force a decision by assault. They apply this concept to defense against amphibious operations, maintaining that combat of this nature is actually offensive in character. Their mission is to annihilate the enemy forces before a landing can be effected or as soon after the initial landings as possible. As one Japanese order expressed this principle, the object of the defense is "to frustrate the enemy's landing plans with a counterattack like an electric shock, and at the proper moment to annihilate the enemy by close-range fire, by throwing hand grenades, and by hand-to-hand combat."

Thus far U. S. forces have encountered Japanese coast defense forces mostly on small islands with vital airstrips, or lagoons utilized as anchorages for seaplanes. Where the island was not large, a perimeter defense was organized, and when this was pierced, the possibility of continued defense of the island virtually disappeared. Where the island was long and narrow, or otherwise unsuited for a perimeter layout, the defense was concentrated within a vital area which was surrounded with tank ditches, barricades, and other obstacles.

The basic problem of coast defense, according to Japanese doctrine, is the shortage of men and fire power inherent in all such operations where the defense has to be dissipated over long coastal strips, while the enemy by his choice of a landing site can bring a concentration to bear at a selected time and place. This problem can be solved in two fundamental ways: The defender can attempt to stop a landing at the shoreline, or he can retain a large mobile reserve and defeat the hostile forces, after the landing, by a counterattack.

The defender can attempt to combine these two solutions, holding the more vital areas in strength and retaining a mobile reserve to cover the less likely landing areas. The Japanese have tried to follow the combination method and can be expected to use it on the shores of their home islands and on the Asiatic Continent. In the organization of the defense of a long shore line they try to anticipate the general areas in which landings will be made by Allied forces, to organize the most suitable landing beaches for strong defense, and to cover the intervening coast with mobile and static patrols.

If Allied troops undertake an attack on the well defended areas of the coast, the Japanese plan to prevent the landing by superior fire power; but, if the landing actually is made despite their efforts, they expect to defeat it at the water's edge with counterattacks by the beach garrison and by mobile reserves located well forward. If the landing is made on a stretch of poorly defended coast, the Japanese anticipate the destruction of these forces by counterattacks made by mobile land reserves held in centrally located areas and by counter-landings.

According to Japanese doctrine, positions should be constructed on high ground immediately behind the shoreline to dominate the beaches by fire power and interdict them to hostile landing forces. Otherwise, the positions will be sited near the water line to engage the landing forces at the critical moment when they are dealing with beach obstacles and their heavy fire power is not available. The defensive positions will be sited to take maximum advantage of terrain and to provide both frontal and flanking fire on the beaches. Artillery is boldly sited, although, thus far, limited expenditure of ammunition and failure to achieve any real concentration of fire have been weaknesses characteristic of Japanese defense against amphibious as well as other types of operations.

Occasionally, the Japanese have withdrawn entirely from the coast and have attempted to base their plans for defense on counterattacks from the interior, and on the holding of naturally strong features of the terrain. Usually this withdrawal has been undertaken because their prepared positions near the shore line were rendered completely or partially untenable by our heavy preliminary air and naval bombardment, rather than because of any fundamental change in their doctrine. However, in a few instances, the decision may have been taken because of the strong cave positions available in the interior of many of the larger Pacific islands. The success that the Allies have had in hitting the Japanese in areas where they were relatively unprepared does not mean that they have given up the doctrine of defense in force of vital areas; it simply indicates that they cannot fortify every foot of landing ground and have been forced to concentrate on areas where they consider it likely that we will land. Allied operations thus far show that these strategic estimates often have been faulty.

In most areas that have been subjected to United Nations landing operations, the Japanese have had ample time to complete their defensive preparations. However, such defenses were not always ready on time. On Saipan, for example, the organization of the island for defense was scheduled to be finished by October of 1944, and at the time of our landings there the work was not as far along as it theoretically should have been. Primarily this failure was due to the shortage of shipping but, had the Japanese desired, the entire job could have been done years before the war began. Such failures indicate a poor strategic appreciation of Allied capabilities. Reports from Leyte indicate that there too the Japanese defenses were incomplete. Unmounted guns were found near empty emplacements, and little effort had been made to construct offshore obstacles or barricades.

Figure 1.—Japanese coast defense gun on Saipan captured before it fired a single round.

Nevertheless, as we move farther into the inner Empire, the Japanese will have had even more time to prepare for our coming, the shipping shortage will be less of a factor, and the strategic necessity of a well-prepared defensive will have been even stronger. Therefore, we shall be safe if we assume that the defense of the beaches on which we land in the future will combine all of the sound features that have been found on the landing grounds we already have used, and the only errors will be those that have been constant factors in the operations thus far conducted.

To date the Japanese coastal defense has been confined largely to the areas of the beaches. In his shore-line defensive positions the enemy has fought largely to the last man, and this fanatical devotion to duty has prolonged, to a measurable degree, the period of the defense and has compensated, to a considerable extent, for the shallow depth of the organized area. Once the beaches were passed, the enemy defense degenerated into last-man defenses of key terrain features and wild banzai charges.

It does not follow that this will be the case in all shore-line defensive operations; rather, in areas where the original garrison of the coastal zone can be reinforced from the mobile reserve, the enemy can be expected to defend in depth until such time as he feels that he has accumulated sufficient force to resume the offensive in superior strength. The movement forward of these reinforcements may be by land or sea, depending on the geographical location and the relative ease of movement over the two media. This type of action appeared to be the enemy plan for the defense of Leyte.

Despite the possibility of additional defense in depth, the Japanese are committed to the defense of the important beach areas and can be expected to organize the vital landing sites in strength comparable to that encountered in the central Pacific, and to attempt to destroy the attacker before he lands, or at the water's edge if the landing is made. In addition to beach defense, operations from now on can expect to encounter better organized and more effective resistance in depth, but an acutal landing on a defended beach will be opposed in the same general manner as heretofore.

Basic Principles

In the Pacific areas where fringing coral reefs are to be found around practically all of the islands, the Japanese based their first line of defense on these reefs. The reefs are commonly an obstacle to the landing craft in themselves, as they lie only a few feet below water level at high tide and are generally exposed at low tide. Even those that can be crossed by shallow-draft landing craft under normal conditions at high tide may become impassable if the wind is strongly offshore and drives back the water to lessen the depth over the reef to less than the draft of the boats. This condition was one of the unfavorable factors encountered at Tarawa.

The Japanese do not trust to the reef alone but strengthen this obstacle with log barricades, coral or concrete tetrahedrons, and waterproof mines. These mines can be detonated by direct contact, by fouling a trip wire, or by remote control from shore positions. In addition, a large quantity of the available artillery is ranged in on the reef. There, because of the slower progress of the attacking forces in that area, artillery fire can do the most damage to them.

The average fringing reef is not, in most instances, a solid ring of coral around the island but is broken in places where wind or water conditions are unfavorable to coral growth. These portions of the reef area are given especial strengthening by the Japanese so far as time and the available materials permit. The sinking of small vessels filled with coral rock has been one method used to close open channels through the reef. The amount of artillery, the normal barrage of which is located in this area, will be larger than that ranged on other portions of the reef, and an increased number of sea mines will be used.

While the main concentration of fire and defense is planned for the reef area, if one exists, Japanese doctrine applies in coastal areas where reefs do not exist such as the China coast, Formosa, the main islands of the Philippines, and the Japanese home islands. On such coast lines, the basic doctrine is still to break up the landing before the enemy craft can reach the shore. Underwater obstacles, land and sea mines, and concentrated artillery fire will still be the main defenses employed by the Japanese.

The exact plan of defense will depend on the topography landward and seaward of the beach. As the larger and more strongly fortified regions are reached, the caliber of the defending guns and the distance at which they can engage our landing units will increase. Flat trajectory weapons will be in the majority, and they will be placed well forward on the beach where they can be brought to bear on the convoy at the maximum range and later laid directly on the landing craft as they approach the beach.

While the Japanese expect to break up any landing attack before it reaches the beach, they realize that landings can be made if the hostile forces are willing to bring sufficient matériel into the action. Increasing consciousness of the inferiority of their air, naval, and artillery support has induced the Japanese to emphasize the destruction of hostile forces after they have landed but before they consolidate their positions and extend their beachheads. They therefore work out in detail the plan for the defense of the beach itself. This defense is built around the regimental and battalion guns which usually are sited in open emplacements (though the 37/47-mm AT gun is often found in closed emplacements), located in a line of strong points dispersed in shallow depth and usually not organized for all-round defense. These strongpoints are either emplacements or pillboxes which generally are constructed of local materials but may be built with reinforced concrete placed over a prefabricated steel base when time and the supply situation permit.

Emplacements and pillboxes are designed to be mutually supporting and are covered by riflemen in fox holes sited around the strongpoints. Positions are connected by communication trenches to permit rapid and relatively safe shifting under rifle fire. To insure a certain amount of protection during the heavy shelling that precedes the usual Allied landing, shelters are constructed under or in the close vicinity of the emplacements and pillboxes. Japanese machine guns usually fire along a final protective line, while the mortars fire against frontal targets. Antitank, antiaircraft (when used against ground targets), and field artillery guns ordinarily fire singly or in small numbers against oblique or enfilade targets. Mortars, in most instances, are sited behind the first available defilade, and the artillery is emplaced well forward, some even on the beach itself, though most of the dispositions are relatively normal.

All weapons are ranged in previous to the assault, and buoys with flags mounted on them are anchored at various points out from the shore to act as range markers. There has been a tendency, however, especially at Saipan, for the individual artillery pieces to fire on the equivalent of a machine-gun final protective line. Guns have been observed placing shells with great rapidity and accuracy in areas of water untraversed by any langing craft. On Saipan, 75-mm guns were so emplaced on the beaches as to fire on the boats as they reached the water line. They were disposed in both covered positions and in shallow, open positions.

The Japanese, however, do not rely on fire power alone to defend the beach. Their doctrine calls for their main infantry and tank forces to participate in counterattacks immediately after hostile forces land. Such counterattacks, of course require close cooperation and liaison with artillery, not only with that of the infantry units but with artillery under the control of higher commanders as well. This necessary cooperation has not been too well effected so far, probably in large measure as a result of the disrupting effect of the prelanding bombardment on mental reactions and communication equipment. To provide personnel for these counterattacks, the Japanese place their reserves farther forward than is considered valid practice in other armies. Strategic concentration points along the beaches that may be used by hostile forces are selected in advance as objectives.

At points where bluffs or cliffs, 15 yards or more in height, are situated immediately back of the coast line, Japanese defensive commanders are instructed to concentrate their strength on high ground to the rear, from which positions they can debouch at a favorable moment to destroy the hostile force by counterattack. Thus far, however, the doctrine appears to be not unreasonable, but the Japanese go on to say that, if the attacker has a firm foothold on the beach, and it is impossible to counterattack with full strength, they will employ small forces to carry out surprise attacks, utilizing heavy cover, night, or dense fog to conceal their preliminary movements.

These small-scale counterattacks have as their primary objectives enemy headquarters, artillery, tanks, and key personnel. Frequently no adequate concentration of personnel and fire power can be built up by the Japanese when their basic plan envisions the frustration of the hostile landing attempt at the shore line. The application of these small-scale attacks against the usually compact front of the early beachhead have resulted in excessive losses in comparison with the results achieved. Tanks, theoretically at least, are held in mobile reserve for counterattack missions at critical times and places, but the practice has fallen short of the theoretical goal because of the inherent weakness of the Japanese tanks *vis à vis* U. S. antitank guns and because of their piecemeal commitment.

A recent development in Japanese defensive doctrine calls for the use of counter-landing units against unopposed enemy landings, in areas where it is impossible to garrison the entire coast, or against beachheads established despite Japanese defensive preparations. These units embark along a quiet section of the coast in such craft as are available and, under naval escort, proceed to the site of the hostile landing to land in the rear of the hostile force. Usually the unit will be transported in destroyers and trans-shipped to smaller landing craft which either are carried on the ships or towed by them.

To achieve the essential measure of surprise, the seaborne movement and the counter-landing usually must be undertaken at night. Obviously, the success of any operation carried out by such a unit will depend on sound training, perfect timing among the various units of the command, and an exact knowledge of the enemy situation. The possibility of the successful employment of these units therefore is not great, but their use must be guarded against in any Allied landing operations.

In contrast to the mobile counter-landing units whose mission is the elimination of an entire beachhead, amphibious assault and infiltration units have been organized. Their mission appears to be to move short distances by sea to strike key objectives within the enemy perimeter such as command posts, vehicles, guns, and supply dumps. The unit is of company size, and its three combat platoons are trained with the primary emphasis for each as follows: (1) hand-to-hand combat, (2) infiltration, and (3) amphibious guerrilla assault. The unit has a large quantity of explosives and demolition material and is issued rafts, waterproof bags, and small cargo tubes which indicate that surprise approach by sea is the favorite tactical method. Operations of such units, or portions of them, have been noted frequently in the Pacific area and their use is likely to increase.

Another new type of Japanese unit, which is used to oppose landing operations, is a platoon composed of strong swimmers whose mission is the night attack of landing craft. There appear to be at least two methods of operation. The first is to swim under water toward the enemy landing craft until they are within grenade-throwing range. The swimmers then surface and throw their grenades, which have a four- or five-second delay, at the approaching landing craft. The second method is for the men to swim toward the landing craft, pushing anti-boat mines before them until they make contact with the boats. These mines are supported by wooden frames connected to the mine by wire, and are of the horn type.

Defense of Attu

The Japanese plan for the defense of Attu was based on a supposedly correct appraisal of the possibilities of an attacking force. They assumed that hostile forces would land in the main bay area (Holtz Bay, Sarana Bay, and Massacre Bay) and would proceed up the valley beds of the streams emptying into these bays. They believed "that there was only one channel along which the American attack could come, and that they had determined that channel infallibly." They accordingly planned a defense to hold the high ground to the rear of each bay area with positions that commanded the flanks and rear of any forces that would advance inland up the valleys. Positions of extreme inaccessibility were prepared for machine guns, mortars, and even field pieces, and in almost every case these commanded effective fields of fire.

Machine-gun positions on slopes and hillsides were individually well sited and prepared, but little effort was made to ensure effective coordination of these positions. Terrain features were exploited to the maximum to bring hostile forces under plunging fire from concealed defensive positions. But in most cases, the Japanese opened their machine-gun fire too soon and failed to search or traverse their weapons sufficiently. Effective close-in defense of machine-gun positions usually was neglected.

Artillery was sited to cover the bays so that no landing boat presumably could reach shore while even one gun was still in action. The dual-purpose guns, in addition to their antiboat mission, were used for antiaircraft protection. Practically no obstacles were erected, for the Japanese apparently believed that the difficult terrain was sufficient to slow down any advance by landing forces.

It is also notable that the Japanese had prepared many positions flanking the beaches in the Holtz Bay area, some of them even facing inward and to the rear. Behind the most satisfactory landing beaches were four successive lines of resistance, with the last at the head of the valley.

The defensive plan failed, because of its inelasticity and the failure to make adequate provision for the unexpected. The U. S. Northern Force took the defenders by surprise and outflanked their carefully prepared Holtz Bay positions, while in the Massacre Bay area the landing forces immediately advanced to high ground which outflanked and dominated the Japanese positions. The quick movement of this force had not been visualized, and no effective countermeasures were devised.

Use of Terrain—Biak

The cave defenses on Biak afforded a striking illustration of Japanese utilization of terrain features in beach defense. Biak island is of volcanic origin, and around the original land mass thus built up, a coral reef ultimately was formed. Successive thrusts raised the land mass from time to time, and additional coral reefs developed in the pauses between such thrusts, forming a series of broken cliffs, rises, and ridges, 8 to 200 feet high. Erosion and subsequent formation of faults and fissures resulted in the creation of a large number of caves.

Along the beaches were caves 3 to 50 feet deep which often gave access to other caverns or to transverse tunnels in the face of the cliff. These caves frequently were utilized by the Japanese for machine-gun emplacements as well as for storage of food and ammunition.

Tunnel-like caverns traversed the bases of narrow coastal ridges, at heights of 20 to 30 feet, with openings in the seaward cliffs. These openings usually were strengthened by concrete machine-gun ports. Such caverns were irregular, approximately 15 to 25 feet long, 8 to 15 feet wide, and 3 to 60 feet high. Personnel entered, and supplies were brought in, through rear openings in the landward faces of the ridges. Machine guns frequently were sited in these caves with fields of fire that usually were exclusively frontal.

Some of the tunnels, however, had their seaward openings masked by aprons consisting of portions of cliffs which had been broken from the main faces by sea action or erosion. Between the cliffs and these aprons were narrow alleys, the ends of which frequently were sealed with concrete and pierced for machine-gun ports.

Figure 2.—Cave used by Japanese in defense of Biak.

Galleries, or series of intermittently connected cavities 4 to 8 feet high and 3 to 6 feet deep, were found at various elevations. Those east of the Parai defile, for example, were 80 feet above the coastal road and 200 yards back from the beach. They were reached by a 75-degree slope of rotten coral. Continuity of the galleries was interrupted by limestone masses or by unions of stalactites and stalagmites, but such obstructions occasionally were bypassed by short connecting tunnels. In the wooded area behind the cliffs a number of mortars were sited, and machine guns were emplaced above the face of the cliff.

On ridges north of the coastal plain there were many holes or faults, circular in shape, 30 to 75 yards in diameter, and 15 to 75 feet deep. The sides of these holes were sheer or very steeply sloped. One or more caves opened from the bases of these holes and were used as personnel and supply shelters. The so-called West Cave accommodated 900 men and contained radio installations and electric lighting. Mouths of these caves often

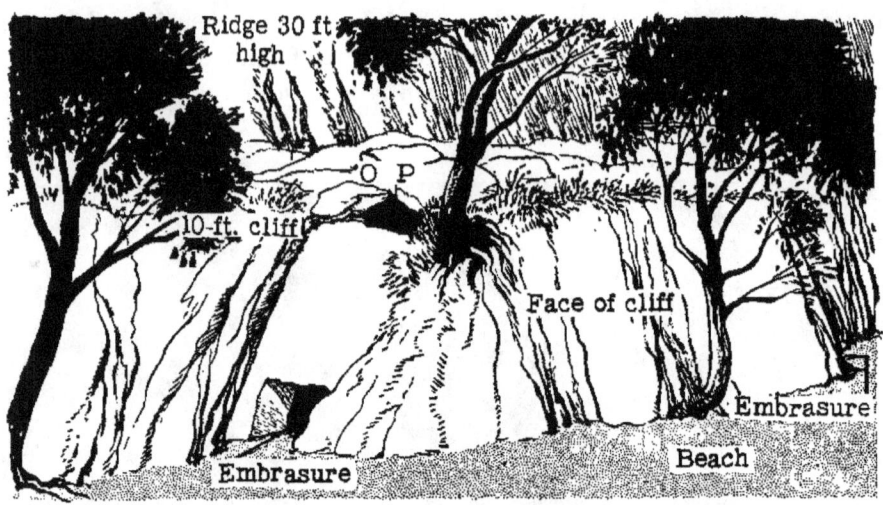

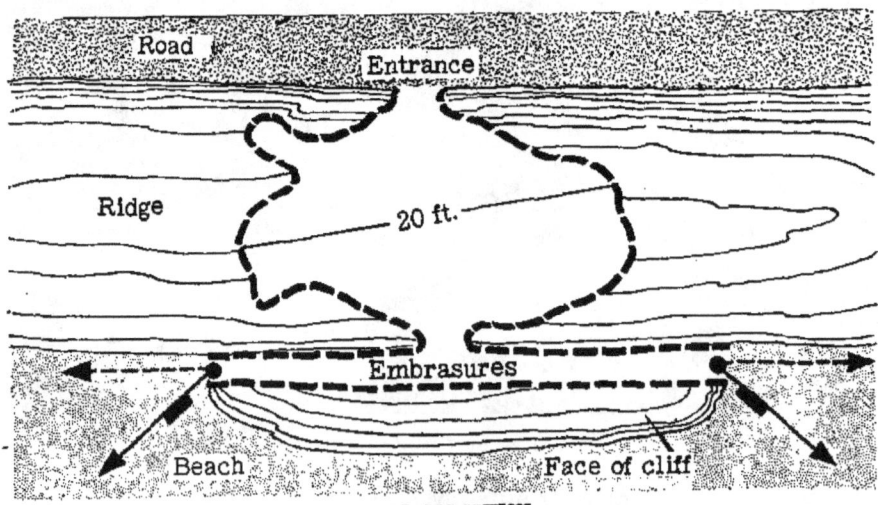

Figure 3.—Japanese observation post on Biak.

were screened by stalactites or stalagmites which, if they did not actually conceal the openings, frequently deflected fire.

Despite the natural advantage presented by the terrain, the Japanese failed to defend Biak successfully, primarily because they predicated their entire defense plan upon their conviction that the caves were invulnerable. They relied too heavily on a passive defense, permitting the American task force to land virtually unopposed and withdrawing their outpost forces

Figure 4.—Coast-defense gun emplacement on Guam.

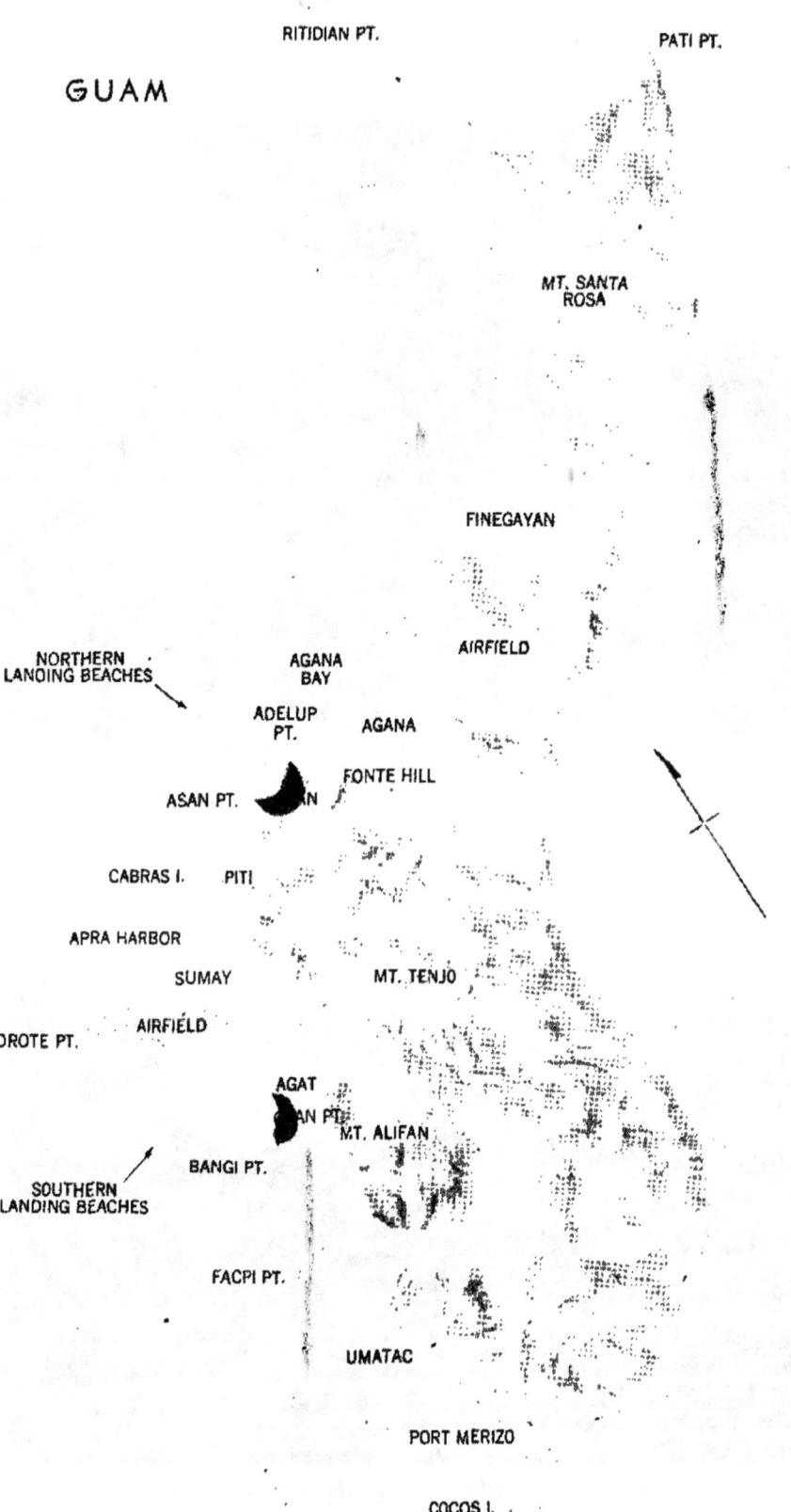

Figure 5.—*Map of Guam showing landing beaches.*

without fighting. Japanese reserves were wasted by piecemeal commitment, and their tanks were sacrificed in disastrous combat with American tanks.

Cave defenses on Guam also were elaborate. One cave, about 60 yards long, and 10 to 30 feet high, was used as a field hospital. The natural cavern had been considerably enlarged by excavation. The hills behind the beaches were honeycombed with artificial caves, reinforced to be shrapnel-proof. They were interconnected by tunnels, and many were used for living quarters. Entrances, in many instances, were barred by reinforced concrete doors.

Figure 6.—*Cave defenses on Guam.*

The Japanese did not fail to utilize other means of defense on Guam. The comprehensive defense plan included coast-defense batteries, antiaircraft batteries, both heavy and light, and a formidable pattern of blockhouses and pillboxes. Buildings on or flanking beaches suitable for landing were skilfully employed as strongpoints, and the beach obstacles alone were so well constructed and sited that no landings could have been made until they had been removed.

Numerous caves along the Peleliu ridges were used effectively by the Japanese for the emplacement of weapons as well as for personnel shelters. Ammunition and food supplies for long periods were stored in the caves and water was obtained from seepage. Entrances to many of the caves

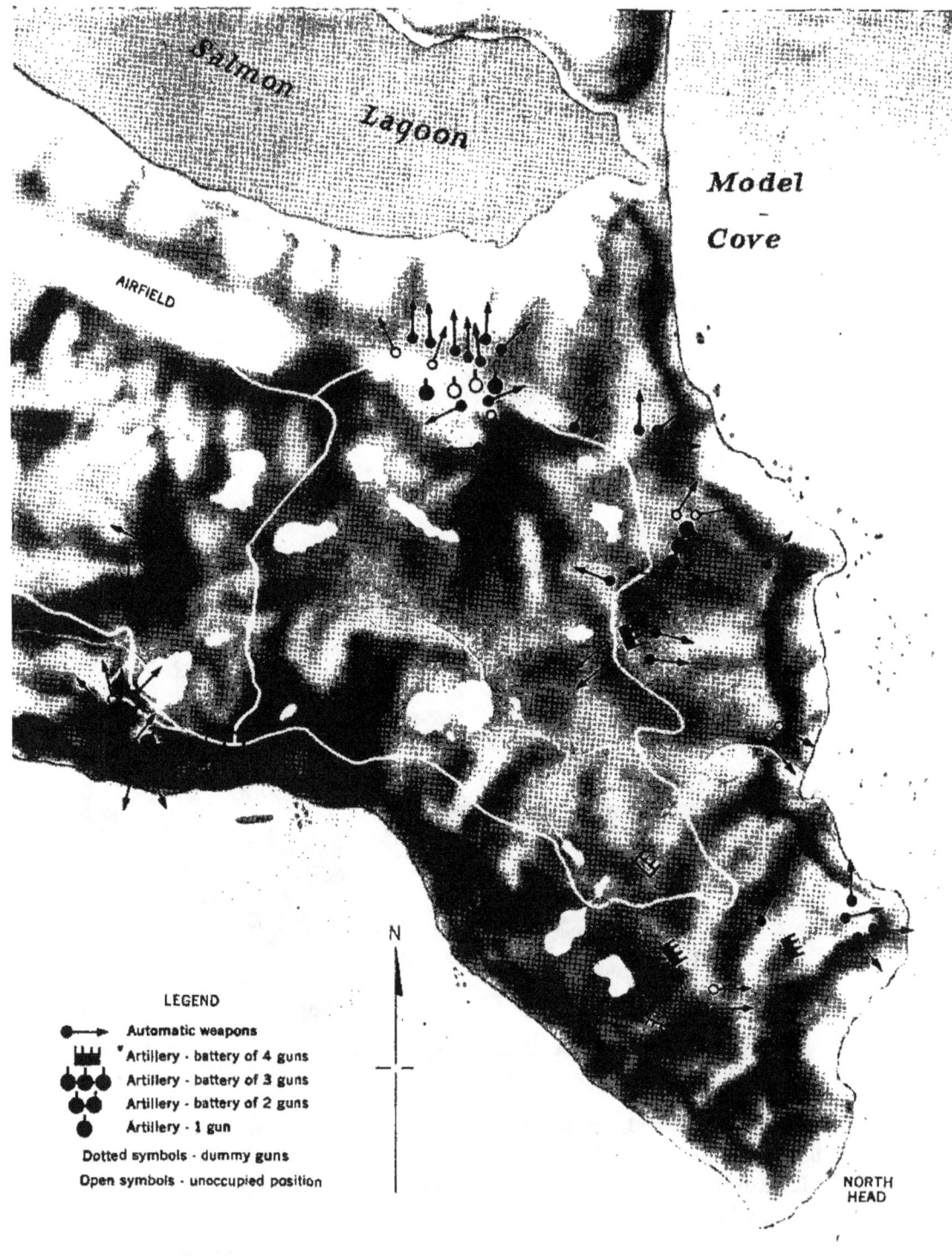

Figure 7.—Map of Japanese defenses on North Head, Kiska.

were barricaded with reinforced concrete, oil drums and barrels filled with stones and gravel, logs, and in some cases steel doors. Bombardment was not very effective against these cave positions, and it usually was necessary to dislodge the Japanese with demolition procedures, smoke, flame throwers, and grenades.

Kiska

On Kiska, the Japanese made excellent use of the rugged terrain, a shore line with steep cliffs with sand or gravel strips at the heads of the coves. Defense installations interdicted the steep stream valleys which rise abruptly between towering hills to high ridges of the interior. Accessible beaches were heavily mined, and tank traps blocked the overland exits from them. Barbed wire was strung between breaks in the line of bluffs, and from the high ground at their extremities the beaches were covered by well-camouflaged and strongly constructed machine-gun positions and rifle pits, with 37-mm and 75-mm guns emplaced in covered positions at a few strategic coves. All artillery except antiaircraft was dug in and covered. All machine guns were connected by underground approaches. One hundred fifty miles of interior roads and trails had been constructed to facilitate the shifting of defense forces.

In contrast, defenses on Attu were not nearly as well developed. There was no road net, and neither water nor power systems were comparable with those on Kiska. While Attu was defended only by 75-mm and 20-mm antiaircraft guns, and 75-mm and 37-mm mountain guns, Kiska, in addition to these, had 6-inch, 4.7-inch, and 76-mm naval coast defense guns, 25-mm and 13-mm single and dual-purpose antiaircraft guns, and 3 light tanks.

Tarawa Atoll

The defensive system of Betio (Tarawa Atoll) "was a small island edition of the German West Wall, with one extremely important difference—no depth," according to a report. An all-round, decisive defense at the beach was planned which would utilize the 13-mm heavy machine gun as the basic beach defense weapon along the north coast and both sides of the eastern tip, while the 7.7-mm heavy machine gun would be the backbone of the defense on both the western and southwestern coasts. The 13-mm machine guns were located in open emplacements to allow their use as antiaircraft as well as ground weapons and were sited to cover most likely approaches between the beach obstacles with frontal fire and the forward side of the diagonally placed barriers on the reefs with flanking fire. Carefully built rifle and light machine-gun emplacements were sited in and immediately behind the beach barricade to provide local protection for the automatic weapons.

Coast defense and dual-purpose guns were mounted carefully in strongly constructed emplacements of reinforced concrete or coconut logs revetted

BETIO

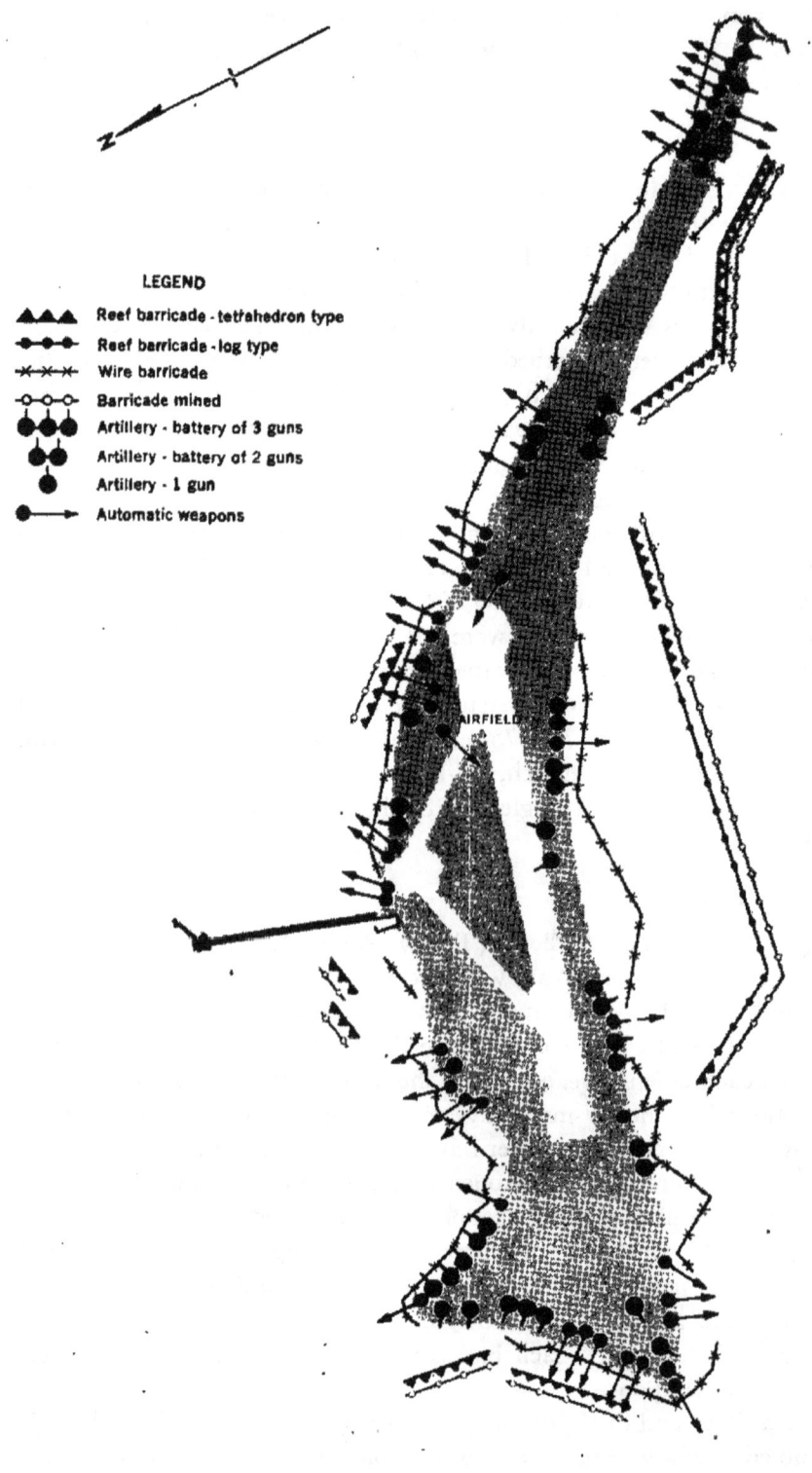

Figure 8.—Map of Japanese defense installations on Betio.

with sand. Personnel, ammunition, and vital supplies were protected from shelling and bombing by sand-covered log and concrete bomb-proof shelters, ordinarily placed opposite, and approximately 30 yards in front of, the interval between pairs of guns. Pillboxes were within 50 yards of the water line and placed at 25- to 50-yard intervals in a line roughly paralleling the beach.

The outstanding weakness of the position was the organization for inshore defenses, which arose out of basic Japanese doctrine and its stress on effecting a decision at the water line. Bomb-proof ammunition and personnel shelters inshore from the beach finally were improvised as defense positions, and the fire from the doorways of these in a number of instances was mutually supporting. This advantage, however, was a

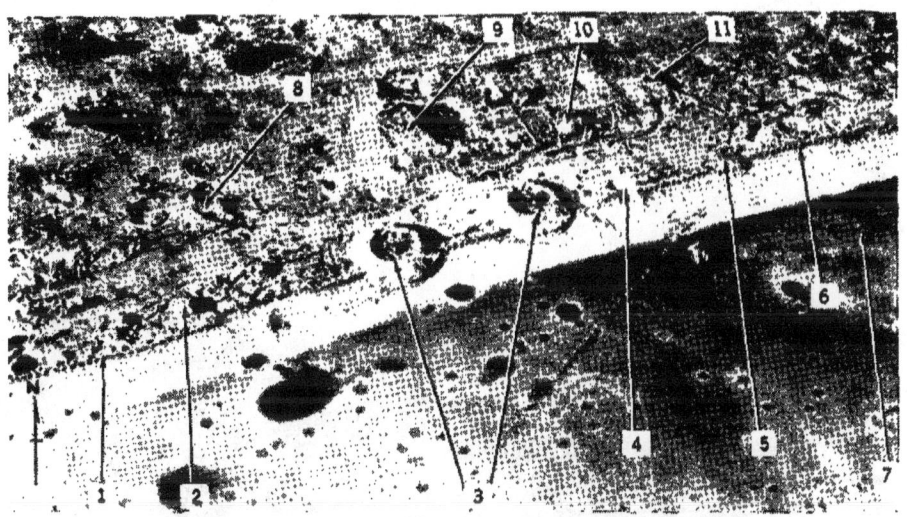

Figure 9.—*Typical shore-line defenses along southwest shore of Betio.* (1) 150-mm searchlight; (2) bombproof shelter; (3) twin-mount 127-mm DP guns; (4) (5) (6) twin-mount 13-mm machine guns; (7) barbed wire; (8) ammunition storage dump; (9) range finder; (10) native building; (11) ammunition storage.

fortunate accident and not the result of deliberate planning. For the most part these improvised defense positions were blind to attack, since they had not been designed as blockhouses and had few firing ports.

Roi Island, too, was organized for the concentration of the defense efforts at the shore line. Five strong, circular concrete pillboxes were built on the sea side. These structures had walls 4 feet thick, and embrasures were protected by ¼-inch steel plates. Inside walls of the pillboxes were lined with 1 inch of rock wool as a protection against moisture as well as to minimize fragmentation.

On Helen Island, of Tarawa Atoll, was one of the most heavily defended areas encountered thus far in the Pacific. Artillery of 3- to 8-inch caliber was skilfully sited and strongly emplaced. There were many concrete and log pillboxes, shelters, an elaborate system of trenches and

Figure 10.—Portion of sea wall on Betio (above); Japanese barricade positions behind sea wall (below).

Figure 11.—Concrete and log defenses on Betio.

machine-gun emplacements, underwater mines, scullies, wire, and log fences.

Kwajalein

Kwajalein defenses, while of lesser strength than those of Tarawa, likewise had an abundance of concrete structures and sturdy beach obstacles. The defense relied primarily upon field fortifications to liquidate ground forces and twin-mount 5-inch double-purpose guns for defense against naval attack. The defense layout consisted of an elaborate trench system, reinforced by concrete pillboxes and by log or log and sand pillboxes. On the lagoon side, landings had been anticipated, and the preponderance of defensive strength accordingly was concentrated on that side. The trenches were in an erratic zigzag pattern, with a depth of approximately 30 yards back of the line of dunes along the shore. Lack of depth was an outstanding weakness, for the distance from one trench to the next behind it was only about 15 yards. The trenches were about 3 feet deep and 2 feet wide, usually unrevetted and dug on high and low ground intermittently.

A comparatively small number of concrete and earth pillboxes were found on this island and these were concentrated on the lagoon side. Along a 500-yard stretch of this coast there were three concrete, two coral masonry, and two log pillboxes, as well as three sandbag dugouts with fire slits and three earth dugouts with a ¾-inch overhead cover. The pill-

Figure 12.—Aerial photograph of Namur Island.

Figure 13.—Coral stone fortifications, Kwajalein.

boxes were sited on a line right on the beach, and they were not laid out for mutual support. Fire apertures were sited mainly towards the water, in conformity with coast defense doctrine and the basic plan. Concrete was employed primarily for the construction of shelters to provide refuge for personnel during aerial and artillery bombardments. Many of these shelters were built on the reverse sides of sand dunes.

When dugouts were covered, the ceiling usually was composed of steel or corrugated iron, $3/4$ to 1 inch thick, covered with a foot or two of earth. A number of tanks were emplaced in revetted ditches as stationary pillboxes.

Munda and Vila

At Munda the Japanese ground defense centered around a system of well concealed, well constructed pillboxes and dugouts, scattered along the coast from Bibile Hill to Laiana and inland for a maximum distance of approximately 1,800 to 2,000 yards.

Likewise, at Vila the majority of defenses were sited along the coastline to guard against frontal assault. From Parapatu Point to Disappointment Cove there were three lines of supporting and automatic weapons emplacements. One 75-mm gun also was found in a covered emplacement.

ENGEBI

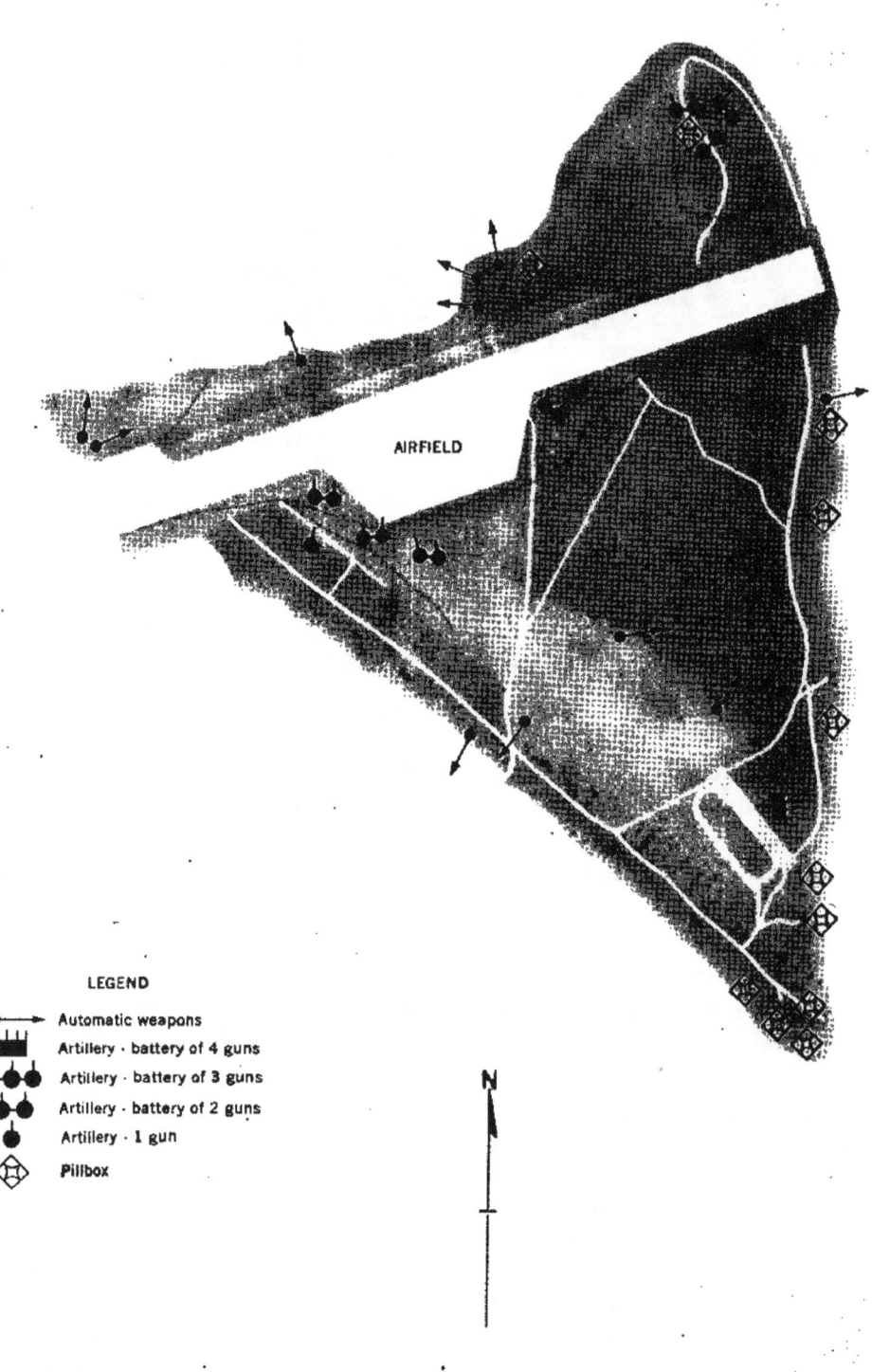

Figure 14.—Map of defenses of Engebi Island, Eniwetok.

Figure 15.—Japanese pillbox on shore line at Munda.

Along the waterline, the positions were not dug in because of the water table and the resultant lack of drainage. The positions were built of coral rock, coconut logs, and sand-filled oil drums. Heavy machine guns wherever possible were sited on relatively high ground. Back from the beach a line of covering positions bordered on the jungle primarily to protect bivouac and supply areas within the forest.

Eniwetok

On Eniwetok, on the other hand, the Japanese relied almost exclusively on field fortifications, and apparently planned to ring the entire island with such fortifications for a perimeter defense. There were many rifle pits, shelters, and trenches, some of which were some distance inland but most of which, in conformity with the general Japanese practice, were within 50 yards of the water line. There were almost no pillboxes or bombproofs, and the use of concrete was extremely meager. Two 4.7-inch Model 1898 British coastal guns were the largest coast defense weapons. However, in view of the progressive program of constructing Japanese defense positions, it is possible that later phases of construction would have included installation of stronger positions.

Makin

The defense plan for Makin envisioned the defense of only a two-mile strip. An important installation was the seaplane base on the lagoon side

Figure 16.—Japanese pillboxes on Kwajalein beach.

Figure 17.—Japanese light tank dug in for defense of Eniwetok.

Figure 18.—Japanese 4.7-inch gun emplacement on Eniwetok.

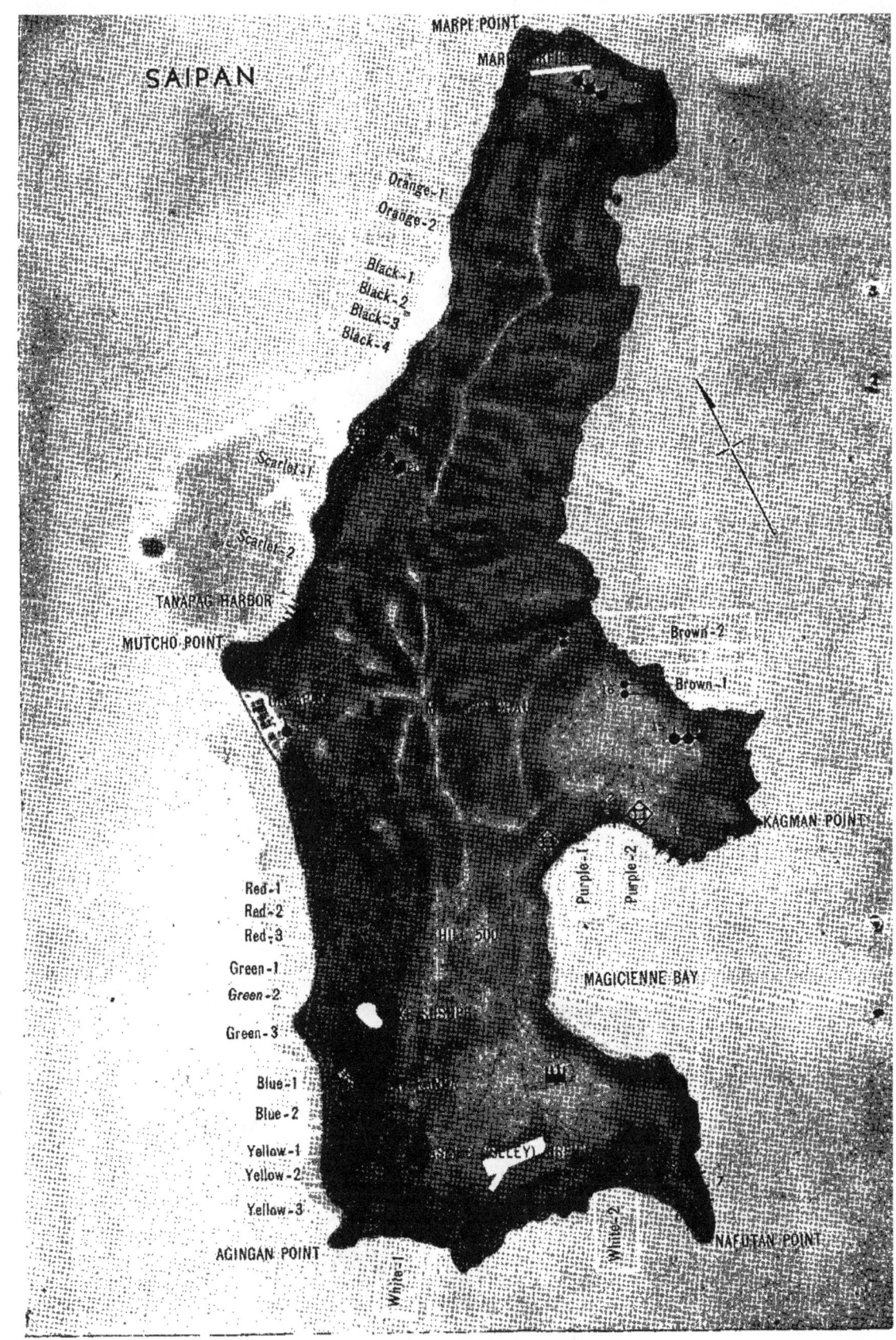

Figure 19.—Map of defenses of Saipan.

along the north shore, and a perimeter defense accordingly was thrown around this. A network of antitank clearings, double-apron and trip wire, tank ditches, as well as antitank and machine-gun positions was constructed. On the north shore, three dual-purpose 80-mm guns were emplaced, together with a few machine guns, while on the south shore there were three 80-mm dual purpose guns, three antitank positions, 10 machine-gun emplacements, and 85 rifle pits. The inner defense was planned as an all-around system whereby support could be provided for points in the outer defenses jeopardized by hostile attack.

Saipan

The defense of Saipan afforded an illustration of a Japanese attempt to employ both their basic alternatives of coastal defense tactics. The plan was to destroy hostile forces before they reached the beach on the east and south shores as well as to deny them Tanapag harbor by linear shore defenses of the type encountered in other island areas. On the other hand, a mobile force was kept in readiness for counter actions against attempts to land on other beaches. The defense plan also was unique in view of the great reliance placed upon boldly-sited and well-emplaced field artillery. A total of 79 pieces of field artillery was found after the U. S. capture of the island. Although field artillery was expected to play a dominant role in the defensive tactics, no horses or prime movers were

Figure 20.—Camouflaged Japanese field piece captured intact on Saipan.

available to assure mobility, a fatal weakness. This probably was attributable to the havoc wrought on Japanese shipping by U. S. naval forces.

The defenses were by no means complete, in all likelihood a result of the unanticipated rapidity of the U. S. advance through the Gilberts and Marshalls. Not a single coastal defense or antiaircraft position was complete. A battery of three 140-mm guns was still loaded on railway cars and twenty-three 120-mm dual-purpose guns were found still in cosmoline, while 36 coastal and dual-purpose pieces still were at the Garapan naval depot when the island was occupied by U. S. troops.

Yet even had the defenses been completed as planned, the over-all defense would have been poorly organized and equipment meager. There apparently would have been a dearth of beach obstacles and land mines, and the poor training of the troops in defensive tactics also would have been a grave weakness.

Figure 21.—Japanese 6-inch gun emplacement on Tinian.

General Estimate

Japanese fortifications in the various defense installations encountered to date have had a number of features in common. Concrete works generally were supported by open earth works. Fieldworks, where they did not constitute the mainstay of the defenses as on Eniwetok, and to a lesser degree on Kwajalein, were used to cover dead areas, to engage enemy forces attempting to assault concrete works, to facilitate the mounting of local counterattacks, and to impart some measure of flexibility to the beach-line defense.

Concrete structures were relatively few in comparison with other types. There has been no apparent relation between the size of concrete structures and the thickness of their roofs and walls. On Kwajalein, for example, a shelter 60 by 11½ feet had a roof and walls only 2 feet thick. Command posts, on the other hand, almost invariably will have very thick walls and roofs. Spacing of concrete pillboxes has varied from site to site and has been irregular within individual sites. On Kwajalein three were sited within 500 yards of each other. No strongpoint has had concrete shelters with sufficient aggregate capacity to protect the entire personnel. No tank turrets have been installed in pillboxes, although on Kwajalein and Saipan buried tanks were used as pillboxes.

Only a few field guns have been found set up in covered emplacements; notably on Kwajalein and Saipan. Both large and small calibers frequently have been found, either in open works or in open-type emplacements. Only a few antitank guns have been installed in concrete emplacements. Coastal guns, on the other hand, have been installed in strong emplacements and have been protected locally by light machine guns.

Some Japanese coastal defense installations overcome by U. S. forces have been well conceived and constructed. They have been well integrated with terrain features; artillery and machine-gun positions have been sited to deliver both frontal and flanking fire on beaches suitable for landing, and at least some attention has been paid to mutual support features of pillboxes and other installations. Obstacles as well as coastal mines, while only moderately effective, have been laid with the object of channeling landing boats into interlocking fields of fire, although intrinsic defects in the obstacles and their installations usually have prevented full realization of the potentialities envisioned by the basic plans.

Considerable fundamental defects have been inherent not only in Japanese tactical doctrine of defense against amphibious operations but also in the application of the doctrine. Since the objective is believed to be the annihilation of the enemy at the water line, the defense installations have been concentrated very near the shore and in almost every case have lacked adequate depth. In the defense of Biak, the Japanese failed to utilize natural features into a well-coordinated defense position. Secondary and switch positions were almost entirely lacking. There were no underwater mines or beach obstacles; and land mines, which were sparsely set, were of poor quality. On the other hand, the caves which constituted the main strongpoints were well stocked; dumps of rations, ammunition, and other necessities were well dispersed and concealed, and adequate fields of fire had been cleared before the caves.

Log and coral pillboxes overlooked Mokmer airdrome from a nearby ridge. There were two concrete pillboxes, and on Bosnek four steel pillboxes had been erected. Four 120-mm naval guns were mounted southwest of the revetment. The emplacement of four 6-inch naval guns had been started but only one was completed at the time of the U. S. attack.

On Noemfoor, however, the fortifications were so crude, according to an observer's report, "as to be classified as puerile. It is inconceivable that any combat troops, supposedly well-trained, could, by the wildest stretch of their imagination, have thought such a fortified position would stand in the face of naval or artillery bombardment."

Organization

In the pre-war Japanese Empire, coast defense fortresses were commanded by officers from the rank of colonel to lieutenant general, depending upon the importance of the installation. These commanders were responsible either to the army district commander or to the army commander of the area involved.

Coast-defense fortifications were manned by units which ordinarily were made up of headquarters, one heavy artillery regiment or battalion, one or more infantry battalions, construction and port engineers, signal units, and antiaircraft units. On Chichijima, a field artillery battalion has been identified, in addition to a heavy artillery regiment, as part of the coast defense force. It is also interesting to note that 13 infantry battalions are under this command.

The heavy artillery unit, which may be either a regiment or a battalion, depending upon the size and importance of the fortress, is the nucleus of the coast defense force, just as the infantry is the basic element of land forces of other types. The heavy artillery unit is the permanent, fixed element, while the infantry complement is subject to considerable variation in strength and is capable of rapid reinforcement in the event of imminent danger of hostile landings. In Japan itself, for example, local coast defense units allegedly can be reinforced by a regiment of infantry within 12 hours, and by a division within 24 hours. Thereafter reinforcements presumably can be sent in at the rate of a division every 24 hours.

Four types of heavy artillery regiments have been identified, at least tentatively. One type has a total strength of 1,533 officers and enlisted men. It is divided into two battalions, each with two companies, and is equipped with a total of sixteen 240-mm howitzers. An approximately half-size regiment, equipped with only 8 howitzers, has a total personnel of 789. Such regiments have no battalion subdivisions but are organized into two companies each.

A two-company regiment of 623 officers and enlisted men also is reported; it is armed with four 300-mm heavy mortars. There also is reason to believe that another type of regiment exists which has two companies, with a total strength of 637 and eight 150-mm guns as its chief armament.

Island-defense personnel may include organizations of the Special Naval Landing Forces as well as army units. These forces were formed, beginning in 1932, primarily for landing operations on the China coast. They were organized into battalions, each of 2,000 men apportioned to four companies. Three of the four companies each had six rifle platoons and a heavy-weapons platoon, equipped either with four 3-inch naval guns or two 75-mm and two 70-mm guns. Tanks and armored cars were attached when expedient.

These forces were intended primarily for offensive operations; one such force took Wake Island, while another seized the Gilberts. As Japan has been forced to assume the defensive, however, the Special Naval Landing Forces are being utilized to an increasing degree for defensive missions. Modifications in their organization and equipment have accompanied the change in the nature of their function. Artillery equipment is being enlarged, in some cases by the inclusion of pedestal-mounted naval pieces. One Special Naval Landing Force was reinforced by the addition of another rifle company with four platoons. Three of these platoons each had 3 light machine guns and a grenade discharger in addition to the rifles. The fourth platoon was a heavy machine-gun platoon equipped with 8 of these weapons.

The First Amphibious Brigade, encountered in the Marshall Islands, was a mobile striking force that the Japanese apparently intended to base on Kwajalein to bolster the defense of any threatened positions in the Marshalls. The brigade had a total authorized strength of 3,940. It had also a sea-transport unit of 1,540 officers and men.

The brigade, which had a headquarters personnel of 118, was divided into 3 battalions, each with a strength of 1,036. Besides the battalions, the brigade had a machine cannon unit with a strength of 76, a tank unit with 66, an engineers unit with 243, and signal and medical units with 139 and 190, respectively. Each battalion, in addition to 3 rifle companies, had an artillery company, a mortar company, and an engineer's platoon.

Each rifle company had 12 grenade dischargers, 12 light machine guns, 2 heavy machine guns, two 81-mm mortars, and a 20-mm automatic cannon in addition to small arms. The mortar company had twelve 81-mm mortars, while three 75-mm mountain guns and two 37-mm antiaircraft guns were allocated to the artillery company. The engineer platoon had a 50-mm mortar, an 81-mm mortar, 2 flame throwers, and demolition equipment. A tank unit with 9 light tanks was under brigade control, as was a machine cannon unit with six 20-mm weapons of this type.

Loss of one island after another before the inexorable advance of Allied naval and land forces, as well as the critical drain on their shipping resources, have impelled the Japanese to organize divisions of a new type for island defense. Divisions for this purpose are intended to be largely self-sustaining, and their localized defense of a particular island is conceived of as an integral part of the strategic perimeter defense of the vast Japanese Empire as a whole. The island divisions are expected to prevent hostile landings, counterattack and destroy such hostile beachheads as may be established despite their defensive efforts, and conduct counterlanding operations.

The *island divisions comprise 3 combat teams, all of which may be* standard type regimental combat teams, or 2 may have standard organization while the third is of the strengthened type. The total strength of an island division is 13,600, but this figure may be raised to 16,700 by inclusion of labor elements which are utilized to exploit to the full the economic resources of the island upon which the division is stationed.

There are a number of pronounced differences between the island divisions and the normal standard or strengthened divisions of the Japanese Army. There is no infantry-group headquarters in the organization of the island division, and a sea-transport unit replaces the transport unit of the normal divisions. The artillery, engineer, and medical units, instead of being under division control, are broken down into regimentally controlled units. There are no cavalry, reconnaissance, or tank regiments in the island division. There is a division tank company, however, and a regimental tank unit in the strengthened infantry regiment if the division includes a regiment of that type. The gun company is expanded, and includes 70-mm howitzers, antitank guns, and, in some cases, 75-mm mountain guns in its armament. Finally, there are organic heavy machine guns in each company of the island division.

CHAPTER II.
Beach Obstacles, Barricades, and Mines

Introduction

In applying the principle of reaching a decision at the shore line or on the beach, the Japanese lay considerable stress on offshore and beach obstacles as a means of wearing down, confusing, and delaying a landing force until a counterattack can be mounted. All obstacles are covered with fire from shore positions, and those installed offshore are sited at points which are easiest for landing craft to pass at ebb tide.

If the slope of the shore is considerable, the Japanese dispose obstacles in depth. If the slope is gradual the obstacles are set back from the shore in order to achieve the height requisite for effectiveness. Utilization of beach obstacles to canalize the movement of landing boats into zones of interlocking fire is recognized as a fundamental objective in achieving a decision at the shore line. On the Tarawa reef, for example, obstacles were erected to force approaching boats into areas swept by antiboat fire from 127-mm, 80-mm, 70-mm, and smaller guns. On Guam, beach obstacles were so well built and adroitly located that, in the words of a U. S. Navy report, "landings could not have been made on either Agat or Asan beaches nor on any other suitable beaches without elaborate but successfully prosecuted clearance operations."

But in some instances, particularly on Biak, no adequate system of beach obstacles was erected; the result was a serious weakness in the over-all defense plan. On Attu there were no obstacles of any sort, probably because the Japanese were confident they could destroy any force that landed when it began to advance up the river valleys.

What the Japanese believe in regard to obstacle construction has been condensed to a considerable extent in the following tables:

Type of obstacle	Effectiveness
Water barges............	They are effective barriers. However, when they are filled, their buoyancy is reduced and, moreover, the freeboard is decreased. Therefore, the Japanese believe, it is best not to use them filled with water since this will lessen their effectiveness.
Pickets.................	Little effectiveness as a barrier.
Wooden barricades.......	Little effectiveness as a barrier.
Barbed wire.............	Effectiveness as a barrier is great. Especially when placed at the water's edge it is difficult for vessels to pass over or through it or to destroy it.
Booms..................	Little effectiveness as a barrier. Vessels are able to pass through. Iron spurs attached to the booms are effective for damaging hulls.
Abatis constructed of tree trunks.	When they have little buoyancy and the water is deep, they have little effect against landing boats. If they are built where the water is shallow, on long and shallow coasts, they will hinder the movements of vessels.
Abatis constructed of tree branches.	They are easily constructed and maintaining them against surf is comparatively easy. They are effective as a barrier against landing troops.
Chevaux-de-frise...........	These obstacles are not easily crossed by vessels.
Floating wire entanglements.	When built in three lines, they are effective and stop the advance of vessels; however, when in two lines, they are ineffective.

Japanese estimate of effectiveness of their beach obstacles.

Type of beach obstacle	Depth of beach obstacle	Personnel		Time (in hrs.)		Special type of tool
		Engineers	Laborers	Preparation	Execution	
Single line wooden barricade	2 lines	1 platoon	160 men	4	25	Man-powered pile-driver.
Double line wooden barricade	1 line	½ of a platoon	200 men	8	30	4 man-powered pile-drivers; 4 electric piledrivers.
Barbed wire	3 lines	1 platoon (less 1 squad)	160 men	4	30	10 man-powered pile-drivers.
Floating booms {Construction	14 7-piece assemblies	1 platoon	80 men		20	
{Installation	2 lines	1 platoon (less 2 squads)	80 men	4	10	
Horizontally laid nets {Construction	Length 200 yds; width 20 yds.	1 platoon (less 2 squads)	70 men		10	
{Installation	10 nets	1 platoon (less 2 squads)	100 men	4	15	

Japanese estimate of time factors in construction of beach obstacles.

Barbed Wire

A number of types of barbed wire entanglements are employed by the Japanese in coast defense. Both barbed and unbarbed wire are used, and the Japanese apparently believe that the wires, except the lower horizontal strand, need not be stretched tightly. However, the efficiency of their wire installations is increased by stretching wires between the main strands to thicken the net.

Tactical wire often is strung as at Tarawa, where double-apron fences were laid diagonally from the beaches in a conventional pattern. Machine guns were emplaced so that flanking fire could be laid parallel to and just ahead of this wire. On Kwajalein, in contrast, the wire was not tactical, but was strung in straight lines parallel to the beach. It was not zigzagged, and often was within grenade range of Japanese positions. On Eniwetok the wire installations were negligible.

On the Betio beach high, double-apron wire also was set up inside a line of tetrahedronal concrete obstacles to canalize assault troops upon disembarkation into trip wire and enfilade fire from heavy and light machine guns. This wire installation survived bombardment, but ultimately was breached by amphibious tractors. Double-apron wire also was strung on Kiska across the mouths of stream valleys. It was from 2½ to

Figure 22.—Barbed wire beach obstacles on Guam.

5 feet high and 10 feet wide. On Roi, a low-wire, double-apron installation was used.

Single-apron wire was strung in front of positions in the log barricade on Betio. It was strung from the tops of vertical logs to stakes driven into the sand forward of the barricade. Low wire was strung to protect covered machine-gun emplacements and to supplement the canalizing effect of the double-apron installation.

Figure 23.—Looking seaward through barbed wire entanglements on Betio beach.

Low entanglements, installed about 1 foot off the beach, were used on Kiska to stall advancing troops; and a four-strand fence, 2½ to 3 feet high, with criss-cross wire between the four main strands, also was strung on the crests of steep bluffs. At Reynard Cove, barbed strands were strung from the top of a 15-foot bluff to pegs driven in the sand of the beach. Along the beach line of Roi a concertina type of barricade was erected.

Concrete Obstacles and Log Barricades

About half of the island of Betio was ringed with concrete tetrahedra, the bases of which were about 3 feet square, embedded midway on the reef where they barely broke the surface of the water at high tide. They were sited to canalize landing boats into fields of fire from antiboat emplacements. Set up 6 to 20 feet apart, they had been made on the island by driving angle iron into the ground and pouring concrete into the forms. Here and there tetrahedra were supplemented by piles of coral rock, and mines were laid between the obstacles of both types. The coral piles (cairns), interspersed with mines, were an important feature of the beach defense on Eniwetok as well as on Betio.

One of the most elaborate log barricades encountered to date was the one that almost entirely surrounded Betio. A portion of this perimeter barricade consisted of a coral-block sea wall, and another portion was made up of tree stumps laid on the ground and facing seaward. The remainder of the obstacle, however, was made up of logs, some sections of which included rifle pits and emplacements. The log barricade, with the coconut logs well-wired and stapled, was strongly built and withstood everything except direct hits by naval shells and heavy aerial bombs.

Figure 24.—Coral and log obstacles on Guam.

On the south beach was an antiboat barricade which was extended by tetrahedron obstacles. The barricade was sited to divert landing boats east and west of the center of the south beach, toward antiboat fire from dual-purpose antiaircraft guns and the flanking fire of heavy machine guns. The barricade, 10 feet high, was in the form of a wide-angle V, with one leg 700 yards long and the other 300 yards. It was constructed of coconut logs, secured in place with wire and ½-inch soft steel staples.

Improvised Obstacles

Improvised obstacles requiring little or no use of imported materials such as concrete, cement, or iron, are likely to be encountered more frequently as Japanese shipping resources become progressively more strained. Their inability to secure imported materials, in some instances, already has made it impossible for the Japanese to complete their defenses. At Saipan, for example, lack of materials prevented them from emplacing some of their available major artillery pieces.

Low oblique photographs show that where the Japanese have been unable to secure iron or concrete, they have relied on rocks, logs, and available barbed wire and nails. Mounds of rocks, 10 to 12 feet square and piled about 3 feet high, have been found, staggered at 10- to 15-foot intervals on the outer edges of reefs. Such mounds may contain mines. Tetrahedra, made with logs and filled with rocks, also have been reported. A variation of a tetrahedron, called a "spider", is constructed of logs or poles, either braced by cross members at the base and weighted with rocks, or anchored with its ends buried in the sand. "Spiders" are spaced at intervals of from 15 to 30 feet, and often are incorporated in wire fences.

Rock walls have been built approximately 4 feet high and 3 to 4 feet wide. In some instances these are topped with wire. On Guam, rolls of

Figure 25.—Wire and log obstacle on Guam.

mesh wire, filled with rocks and arranged in a line along the outer edge of a reef, were improvised as beach obstacles.

There also is evidence that the Japanese are prepared to utilize rows of gasoline or oil filled drums which can be electrically ignited to check landing attempts. Calcium phosphide apparently is used as an igniting agent which assists the spread of the gasoline or crude oil after it is aflame.

Tank Barriers and Traps

Japanese defense plans take account of the probability that hostile landing forces may attempt to put light or amphibious tanks ashore, and obstacles and barricades of various types are erected to stop or retard such attacks. When concrete tetrahedra or coral cairns are intended to stop tanks as well as boats, they are put about 6 feet, 7 inches apart, and they may be set up in several staggered rows. Rough stone obstacles, 2½ to 3½ feet high, with a trapezoidal cross section 20 inches at the top and 28 inches at the bottom, may be used in a similar fashion. Large, heavy posts in rock bases also may be installed at about the same intervals.

On the lagoon side of Kwajalein, an antitank barrier was erected which consisted of two horizontal steel rails, weighing 25 to 30 pounds per yard and wired to 10-inch posts set 8 to 10 feet apart.

On another beach, an intermittent wall of concrete or masonry, 3 feet high and 2 feet thick, was erected. Along some sections of the wall there were firing slits to permit use of the structure as a rampart. Occasionally wooden posts were set in the wall, either in a vertical position or at an angle of as much as 45 degrees. These posts protruded 3 to 6 feet ahead of the line of the wall. Along some sections wire was strung between the posts.

Antitank ditches also have been found as integral parts of Japanese coastal defenses. On Tarawa, the ditches were shallow because of the nature of the water table. They were 5 to 7 feet deep, and 12 to 14 feet wide. Only one ditch was revetted, and this exclusively on one side. Wire road blocks were set up at the junction of roads and tank ditches, and covered machine-gun emplacements were located at each end of the ditch from which antitank fire could be delivered from 37-mm, 70-mm, and 75-mm guns. There also were some antitank ditches for the protection of the south beach of Tarawa. One was 10 yards inboard of the stump barricade and was swept by direct fire from covered machine gun emplacements and open 37-mm gun positions.

A rectangular cross-section ditch was dug diagonally across Kwajalein, 12 feet wide and 6 to 7 feet deep. A similar ditch was under construction on Privilege Island at the time of the U. S. attack. An antitank ditch near one of the landing beaches on Leyte had an average width of 25 feet, with a depth of 3 to 4 feet below ground level and sides built up

Figure 26.—Tank trap just off a Betio beach.

3 to 5 feet. Aside from the ditches thus far encountered, Japanese defense doctrine describes ditches 6 feet, 7 inches in depth, with a trapezoidal cross-section 13 to 16 feet across the top and 6½ feet across the bottom. If such a ditch is dug on a descending slope of from 15 to 30 degrees, an earth rampart is set up a little ahead of the ditch. On an ascending slope of more than 15 degrees, the earth is cut away for about 10 feet into the side of the incline. No attention presumably is paid to slopes of more than 30 degrees, for the Japanese believe that armored vehicles cannot negotiate steeper slopes.

Mines

Extensive Japanese flotation mine fields encountered off Palau indicate that in the confined waters around the Philippines and the China Sea sharply increased Japanese attention to this phase of defense can be anticipated.

Prior to the invasion of the Carolines, very few Japanese sea mines were encountered. Although a U. S. destroyer suffered damage from a mine off Kiska, only a handful of mines were found off the Kiska coasts. All told, less than 200 sea mines were swept up by Allied forces prior to the Palau landing, and these were not very effective. In the waters off the Carolines, however, the Japanese made wide use of moored contact mines. Off Angaur and Peleliu, fields were laid within 300 yards of the shore, and with sweeping still incomplete, 323 mines have been swept out of Kossol Passage, important Japanese anchorage in northern Palau.

Antiboat mines have been utilized by the Japanese in several shore defense installations. Off Betio they were placed between the wire obstacles and the shore, and a number also were set between the concrete-tetrahedron obstacles. These mines were the Model 96 (1936) which are all-welded steel construction in the shape of hemispheres. Two horns containing vials of acid are attached to the casing. When either horn is bent, the acid vial is broken, permitting acid to drop upon the plates of a small battery which has a zinc cathode and a copper anode. A current of sufficient amperage is generated to explode the charge in the bottom of the hemisphere.

A single-horn type also is in use. It weighs about 52 to 62 pounds and is about 14 inches in diameter at the base. The body, which contains about 20 pounds of explosive, is of welded-steel construction. One form is in the shape of a truncated cone, while another that has been reported is bell-shaped. The firing mechanism and method of operation are the same in all models. The single-horn version seems to be easier to manufacture and assemble than the double-horn type, and when used as a land mine it can be buried deeper to avoid detection.

These single-horn mines were used extensively by the Japanese on the Tinian beach. Fifteen were removed by U. S. engineers on D-day, after others, undetected, had caused considerable damage. All of them were buried between the high and low water marks, thus making them a hazard to both landing craft hitting the beach at high tide and personnel going ashore from LVT's at low tide. Some mines were buried to horn depth and had trip rods wired to the horns.

About 50 horned antiboat mines were used by the Japanese as antitank mines in their defense of Gasmata airdrome. The mines were not laid in a regular pattern, but nevertheless were located to give adequate coverage to the area defended. Two groups of seven mines, 216 feet apart, were found, but the rest of the mines were set singly. All the mines were set to be detonated by contact, but some could be detonated electrically from a central switch. The tactical purpose of the mines was to deny the airfield to Allied vehicles and aircraft, but adequate attainment of this objective was precluded by the poor concealment of the mines.

Another mine encountered in coast defense systems is the Model 93 (1933) land mine which has been found laid in patterns of diagonal rows, usually 30 inches apart. A field of 30 such mines was located on a hillside on Kiska, and two rows of them were laid along one of the Attu beaches. This mine, called the tape-measure mine because it resembles a rolled-up steel tape measure, is 6¾ inches in diameter, 1¾ inches thick, and 3 pounds in weight. Its explosive content is 2 pounds of picric acid. The fuze is covered by a brass plug in the center of the top of the casing.

There are loops on the casing to permit suspension of the mine by a cord, or to enable it to be drawn by an attached cord across the path of a tank. Pressures of from 70 to 200 pounds on the plug will activate the mine; variation in detonating pressure is accomplished by regulating the shear wire.

Recently, as the Japanese have become increasingly conscious of the ineffectiveness of the tape-measure mine, even against unarmored vehicles, various expedients have been utilized to reinforce the charge. One procedure is to place two of the mines back to back. Timbers then are placed against the projecting fuzes, and the double unit then is buried atop eight pounds of high explosive. Another method is to bury a magnetic mine over a 150-mm projectile. A Model 93 mine then is placed over the magnetic mine, and its explosion detonates the more powerful charges beneath it.

The principal antitank mine used in defense installations has been the Model 99 (1939) armor-piercing mine, sometimes termed the "magnetic antitank bomb" or "armor-piercing grenade". It consists of a circular canvas bag, 4¾ inches in diameter and 1½ inches thick, containing eight sections of TNT wrapped in wax paper. Four magnets are attached to the outside of the bag. To prepare the mine for firing, a wooden plug is pulled out, and a percussion igniter of the delay type inserted. The mine then is thrust against the tank to which it adheres by reason of the magnetic action. A sharp blow on the fuze cap depresses the firing pin, activating the igniter and producing detonation within 4 to 5 seconds.

Chapter III

Fortifications and Airfields

Concrete Installations

Construction Methods

The Japanese utilize concrete to a varying degree in the construction of blockhouses, casemates, pillboxes, and other types of strongpoints. There is an evident trend, however, to employ concrete more extensively and to enhance the strength of fortifications thus constructed. On Saipan, for example, four steel-reinforced concrete pillboxes, larger and stronger than any previously encountered, constituted important elements in the defense of the vital Aslito airfield. These flat-topped structures were about 50 feet square and 15 to 20 feet above ground.. Each pillbox had but one door, and this was of heavy steel construction. Flame throwers and light artillery were used to no avail against these structures, which could only be reduced by naval gun fire. Surprisingly enough, the pillboxes were not camouflaged, and since they therefore were visible from warships, the task of bombarding them effectively was relatively simple.

The Japanese classify concrete defense installations into four categories on the basis of their resistance to shell and bomb hits. Class "A" structures, which have concrete walls with a minimuim thickness of 2 feet, 7¾ inches, will withstand a direct hit by a 6-inch shell or a 220-pound bomb, according to their computations. Class "B" structures have walls 19.7 inches thick and withstand a 4-inch shell or a 110-pound bomb. "C" structures, with walls 11.8 inches in thickness, can withstand a 30-mm shell, while "D" class are impervious only to light shell fragments and machine-gun fire since their walls are but 3.1 inches thick.

Japanese documents set forth a number of principles which govern the erection of concrete defensive structures. About 18.75 pounds of cement are used to every cubic foot of concrete. When gravel and crushed stone are mixed with the cement, the proportions are 1 cement: 2 sand: 4 gravel or crushed stone; if coral, gravel and sand are used the proportions are 1 cement: 3 coral: 3 gravel: 5 sand. Concrete sections that have to be poured on the spot are reduced to a minimum by the use of prefabricated sections wherever these can be made available.

Figure 72.—Rear view (above) and inside wall of heavily constructed concrete pillbox (below).

In the reinforcement of concrete, steel rods, about .6 inch in diameter, are set into domes and walls of all structures in a criss-cross pattern, usually at a distance of 2 inches from the inner side. The bars will be spaced 7¾ to 11¾ inches apart in each direction. When the material is available, another layer of criss-cross rods is installed near the outer side of the concrete, and the two steel reinforcement layers are linked together with three-strand reinforcing rods. In prefabricated concrete sections, number 8 steel wire ordinarily is used for reinforcement at 7¾-inch intervals. An observation post on Saipan had extremely heavy steel reinforcement for the concrete, consisting of 5-inch pipe and steel rods 1½ to 2 inches in diameter.

Besides steel-bar or wire reinforcement, additional protection against fracturing of concrete structures is afforded by building them partly below ground level, by banking the sides and covering the tops with earth or sand, and by inner wall linings of rockwool or asbestos.

In a number of instances tests have shown the concrete utilized in Japanese defense structures to be of poor quality. The ratio of water to cement, on occasion, has been too high, and the failure to make continuous pours likewise has contributed to structural weakness. The use of salt water in mixing and the failure to maintain uniformity of mixtures are additional reasons for the inadequacy of Japanese concrete. Definite planes of cleavage have been found at pour lines, notably in the large blockhouse on Tarawa. Steel reinforcement bars and their tie-ins have been improperly lapped, and construction joints often are not keyed. The use of coral-beach sand also is believed to be responsible for failure to realize the full potential strength of concrete in defense installations.

Blockhouses

Concrete blockhouses, both rectangular and circular in plan, were constructed on Saipan. One rectangular blockhouse, 28 feet long and 26 feet wide, was located about 400 yards southeast of Agingan Point. It contained one gun compartment, fitted with a single embrasure suitable for a 20-mm antitank gun, and was sited to fire on a landing beach. Another rectangular structure was sited between two massive boulders and concealed by trees. It was 18 feet long and 16 feet wide. The reinforced concrete roof was 5 feet thick, and the walls 3½ feet. The single gun compartment and embrasure were suitable for a 20-mm gun. Another almost square structure was 38 feet 3 inches by 36 feet 6 inches. It was 9 feet 7 inches high, and the reinforced concrete roof and wall were 2 feet 7 inches, and 3 feet thick, respectively. There was one turret, and the blockhouse had a total of 5 firing embrasures.

A circular-type blockhouse, also intended for 20-mm guns, was located about 100 yards from the shore line. It was 40 feet in diameter and had four embrasures. Another circular structure had a diameter of 36 feet 4 inches, and a height of 9 feet 7 inches. The reinforced concrete roof

Figure 28 (a).—Rear view of heavy concrete circular pillbox on Roi. Note camouflaged communications trench.

Figure 28 (b).—Closeup of the circular pillbox shows the steel embrasure lining and cover.

was 2 feet 7 inches thick, and the walls had a thickness of 4 feet. There was a cupola on the roof which was covered with about a foot of earth. The ceiling and walls were lined with a layer of asbestos, 1 inch thick, which served to provide protection against moisture and heat as well as to curb fracturing of the concrete. There were five embrasures suitable for machine guns.

Pillboxes

Aside from the square concrete pillboxes on Saipan, a number of other pillboxes of reinforced concrete construction, both circular and rectangular, have been encountered in operations to date. On Roi Island, a circular pillbox, with a diameter of 40 feet, was 8 feet high and had a wall 4 feet in thickness and a roof 2½ feet thick. The wall was wainscoted to a height of 2 feet and covered with a 1-inch layer of rockwool. There were four steel-faced embrasures, and the structure had a single turret. The reinforcement of the concrete consisted of 4 rows of double 1-inch steel bars, placed in crisscross pattern at intervals of 6 inches.

A combination pillbox and shelter on Kwajalein was 13½ feet long and 12 feet wide. The roof, 12 feet above the floor, was 10 inches thick, and the walls were 8 inches thick. A 1-foot layer of earth covered the top.

Figure 29.—Camouflaged wall with rifle embrasures. Several such walls were found on Guam.

There was only one firing embrasure. Concrete reinforcement consisted of two layers of ½-inch steel bars placed 8 inches apart in crisscross fashion.

Also on Kwajalein the Japanese built a concrete pillbox approximately 11 by 11 by 6½ feet with walls and roof a foot thick. Connected with this pillbox was a concrete ammunition shelter 16 by 16 by 8 feet.

An octagonal reinforced concrete pillbox on Guam was 6½ by 6½ by 5 feet. Its roof was 10 inches thick, and the walls were 8 inches in thickness. This type of pillbox usually was built at crossroads and road junctions. Each installation of this type had 7 small embrasures to permit fire in all directions.

A concrete pillbox on Makin had a domed roof. Its ground plan was square (11 by 11 feet), and it was 5 feet high. The roof varied from 12 to 18 inches in thickness, and the walls were 1½ feet thick. About 2 feet of earth covered the roof, which was sodded for concealment of the installation.

A reinforced concrete pillbox found south of the Leyte airfield was practically identical with those on Saipan and Kwajalein. It had reinforced concrete walls 4 to 5 feet in thickness. It was well camouflaged with natural materials and even had a garden growing on its roof.

Figure 30.—Wrecked reinforced concrete emplacement for 6-inch gun on Saipan.

Casemates

Concrete also has been used extensively by the Japanese in the building of casemates for the emplacement of artillery pieces. On Saipan, a 6-inch gun was emplaced in a reinforced concrete casemate 32½ feet long and 29½ feet wide. The walls were 3 feet thick, and the roof, which was not covered with earth or sand, was 4 feet 2 inches thick. There was one embrasure with an iron cover. An emplacement for a 20-mm cannon was 17 feet 7 inches long, 16 feet wide, and 10 feet high. The roof was 5 feet thick, and the walls 3 to 3½ feet. A similar casemate had large rocks around the embrasure to a depth of about 2 feet.

A concrete casemate for a 75-mm howitzer on Kwajalein was 17 feet long and 19 feet wide. The roof, 6 feet 10 inches above the floor, was a foot thick and was covered with 2 feet of earth, the walls were 14 to 16 inches thick.

Shelters

Bombproof shelters are used by the Japanese primarily as refuges for personnel during aerial and artillery bombardments and for the protection of ammunition and other vital supplies. Many of these are of concrete construction. From observations of covered emplacements on the Gilberts, Marshalls, and Wake Island, it seems that the Japanese have been using more personnel shelters than pillboxes. This is probably a reaction to American air raids on their island positions and may be an indication of what to expect in the future. In addition to affording protection for personnel during bombardment, shelters are used as command posts and medical aid stations. In many cases they serve as standby shelters for troops waiting to man their defense positions or to initiate a counterattack. On Saipan, a concrete shelter for the crew of a 120-mm dual purpose gun, built in the shape of a square 18 feet on a side, was 8 feet 10 inches in height. The walls were 2 feet thick, and the roof 2 feet 10 inches.

The strongest concrete structure on Betio was the so called "Air Defense Command Post", a two-story reinforced concrete building that served apparently to house headquarters personnel and to store certain items of equipment. Although the building had apertures for rifle and automatic-weapon fire, it was not intended to be used as a defense strongpoint.

The building was 58 feet, 10 inches long, and 39½ feet wide. It was 22 feet, 3 inches high, and the ceilings of both stories were 6¼ feet high. The reinforced concrete walls and roof were 3 feet in thickness, and a layer of sand, about a foot thick, covered the roof as antiaircraft defense. The structure was so strongly built that it withstood direct hits by all types of artillery shells without sustaining serious damage, and its ultimate reduction could only be accomplished by flame throwers, grenades, and dynamite. A somewhat similar structure recently found on Leyte had a reinforced concrete roof 5 feet thick.

Figure 31.—Views of "Air Defense Command Post" on Betio.

Another very large shelter, on Kwajalein, was 60 feet long, 11½ feet wide, and 9 feet, 6 inches high. Roof and walls were 2 feet thick, and the door was made of steel plate 1 inch in thickness. The concrete was reinforced with ¾-inch steel bars.

A concrete magazine and possible personnel shelter on Tarawa was 34 feet, 8 inches long, 17 feet wide, and 5 feet, 8 inches high. The roof was 5 feet, 8 inches thick and the walls about 1 foot. An interesting variant of the same type of concrete magazine had a six-sided pillbox on top.

A thirty-man shelter described by the Japanese is 19 feet, 8 inches long, 16 feet, 9 inches wide, and 8 feet, 7 inches high. Walls and roof are 20 inches thick. The shelter was designed to provide sleeping facilities for 14 men in a tier of upper and lower bunks.

The bombproof shelter on Burton Island was 50 feet long and 6 feet wide. The arched roof had a maximum height of 6 feet, and the walls were 4½ feet thick. One-inch steel bars, criss-crossed and 9 inches apart both ways, were installed in both inner and outer faces of the walls. It is interesting to note that shelters under construction were even thicker.

One of the largest concrete shelters encountered thus far was on Namur Island. It was 59 feet long, 25 feet wide, and 10 feet, 10 inches high. Walls were 2½ feet thick, and the roof 2½ to 3 feet. Concrete reinforcement consisted of ⅝-inch steel bars 4 inches apart. On Kwajalein, a shelter 21½ by 15 by 11 feet had a roof 3 feet thick and walls 2 feet thick. Five feet of earth and coral were piled on top the roof. One-inch steel bars, criss-crossed at 8 inch intervals both ways, constituted the reinforcement for the concrete.

Small firing positions seldom are made entirely of concrete, but on Kwajalein a concrete sniper's post was found, 5 feet, 3 inches long, 4 feet, 4 inches wide, and 6 feet high. The roof was 6 inches thick, and the walls 6 to 12 inches. Reinforcement of the concrete comprised ⅜-inch steel bars, laid criss-cross, 6 inches apart both horizontally and vertically. There was one firing embrasure.

Concrete-Covered Steel

Concrete-covered steel pillboxes also have been encountered. At intervals of about 300 yards around the perimeter barricade on Betio there were a number of prefabricated steel pillboxes in the form of truncated hexagonal pyramids. These had double walls of steel, each ¼-inch thick, with the space between them filled with sand. The exterior was banked with sand and camouflaged. Apparently these structures were designed to be covered with concrete, for one was found capped with a layer of concrete 1 foot thick. The pillboxes of this type have an upper and lower compartment. The lower compartment is used for the emplacement of two light machine guns, which on Betio were used to deliver flanking fire.

Figure 32.—Exterior and interior views of Japanese steel pillbox encountered on Betio.

The top compartment is for observation and fire control, and is in communication with the lower compartment by means of a speaking tube.

Prefabricated Concrete

Small concrete defense installations sometimes are prefabricated. A 6-man shelter, 5 feet, 9 inches long, and 4 feet, 5 inches in both width and height is made with 4 cylindrical concrete slabs which are joined on top and bottom by dome-shaped slabs. A precast observation post and light machine-gun shelter has been described as being 3 feet, 11 inches in diameter and 5½ feet high. Wall and roof were each 3 inches thick, and there were three embrasures.

Non-Concrete Installations

Non-concrete installations also have constituted important parts of all defensive systems encountered thus far. On Tarawa, large personnel shelters, located in barracks and headquarters areas, were designed to furnish protection for personnel during air or surface bombardment. These structures, usually large, were built of alternate layers of logs and sod, with the thickness of walls and roofs averaging 5 to 7 feet. Some were provided with ventilation shafts, but were not equipped with gun or rifle ports since they were not intended for active defensive roles.

Shelters

In the vicinity of gun and machine-gun positions standby shelters were constructed as refuges during bombardment. Numbers of these were of concrete construction; many, however, were of log and sand. In the later stages of the fighting on Betio, these shelters were employed as improvised defense positions. They averaged 20 to 40 feet in length and 8 feet in width.

Bunkers

Where the water table is too close to the surface to permit the erection of defense positions that are partially underground, the Japanese construct bunkers. Those built for the defense of Buna were especially formidable. A shallow trench, from 10 to 40 feet long, depending upon the size of the bunker to be built, was dug as a base. A framework of log columns and beams then was erected, and the walls subsequently were revetted with logs as much as 1½ feet thick. A ceiling of two or three courses of logs was laid over the roof beams. The walls then were reinforced with sand-filled oil drums and ammunition boxes, as well as log piles and rocks. The structure finally was covered as completely as possible with earth and sand in which there were many short log lengths. The bunkers, 7 to 8 feet high, were covered with jungle vegetation for camouflage and were extremely difficult to detect.

Bunkers usually are used primarily as shelters during aerial and artillery bombardments and are connected by communication trenches to rifle pits, machine-gun emplacements, and other fire positions. They have, however, fire slits for machine guns and rifles usually about 4 feet long and 8 to 12 inches high, just above ground level.

Double-bay bunkers also are built by the Japanese and may be encountered as inland defensive installations. They have been found in two sizes—25 by 15 feet and 60 by 40 feet. Such bunkers consist of mounds of earth, 5 to 12 feet high, with a rear entrance deeply recessed into them. In front, a central, solid block of earth is left projecting to form a bay on each side of it.

Pillboxes

On both Kwajalein and Eniwetok a number of pillboxes of log and sand construction were found which failed to provide adequate resistance to fire. The logs were often soft and spongy, and caliber .30 rifle bullets penetrated some which were 12 inches in thickness. Various ways of joining the logs were employed. Some were tied by wire, while in other cases they were secured by cleats. Notching and recessing at intervals also were resorted to, and in some installations the logs simply were driven into the ground side by side. Pillboxes located inland from the shore line frequently failed to afford adequate fields of fire, and camouflage was not up to the usual Japanese standards.

Yet on Betio an average of fifteen 75-mm shells were required to penetrate a log pillbox. In tests conducted in the Southwest Pacific Area, an

Figure 33.—Log pillbox, Buna.

average of 8 rounds from a 7.2-inch T40 multiple rocket launcher, fired at close ranges, were necessary to destroy coconut-log pillboxes. British tests have shown that the effect of 3.7-inch howitzer shells is negligible, and that about four hits from a 5.5-inch gun are needed to destroy a pillbox built of coconut logs by Japanese methods.

Pillboxes have been built that utilized sand or earth-filled oil drums along with logs and sandbags. Such an installation on Munda was 6 by 5 by 4 feet. One layer of logs comprised the roof, and the sides were made of a row of 55-gallon drums filled with sand. The sides were reinforced by sandbags and logs.

Figure 34.—Gunport in Japanese log and sand pillbox on Betio.

A log and gasoline-drum pillbox also was part of the defenses of Finschhafen. Seventeen feet long, the installation was 4½ feet wide and 6 feet high. It was constructed of coconut logs and 44-gallon drums filled with sand. The same defense system contained several defense installations built of logs and tin. The roof was built with two layers of logs, and the sides were formed of earth and sandbanked sheet tin. Dimensions of the structure were 27 by 3½ by 4 feet; a variant of this type was only 15 feet long.

Several pillboxes found intact after the American landings on Leyte were built of coconut logs and sand, lined in part with galvanized sheet iron. Rough boards framed the embrasures, which were so located that they covered the beach from an oblique angle of approximately 30 degrees from the shore line and had no direct opening on the beach.

A number of magazines on Saipan were of log construction with concrete and metal reinforcement. One for a 6-inch gun was 27½ feet long by 6½ feet wide, with a height of 6 feet, 4 inches. Walls had a maximum thickness of 6½ feet. A similar structure for an 8-inch gun was 27 feet, 2 inches long, 13 feet, 3 inches wide, and 11 feet high. The roof was 4½ feet and the walls 2½ feet thick. A magazine for a 120-mm coast defense gun was 22 by 23½ by 7 feet. The walls were a foot thick and built of coral rock held by 4- to 6-inch log braces. Another ammunition magazine was 22 by 16 by 7 feet. Timbers, 6 to 8 inches thick, supported the roof which was 4 feet thick and composed of alternate layers of sand and grass. The walls were made of coral rock held in place by log cribbing.

On both Tarawa and Makin log shelters for 37-mm guns were built. They were about 22 by 13 by 4 feet. The roofs were supported by steel I-beams and covered with about 2 feet of earth. On Makin, emplacements for 37-mm antitank guns and 70-mm infantry guns were built with walls of log about 30 inches thick. The structures were 15 feet square and about 4 feet high. Concrete reinforcement, about 15 inches thick, protected the embrasures.

Camouflage and Dummy Positions

Japanese camouflage encountered in amphibious operations thus far has varied greatly in ingenuity of conception and attention to detail. Many fortified positions were camouflaged with such skill and minute care that they were extremely difficult to locate. On Guam, for example, coconut log pillboxes eluded accurate location at distances beyond 20 to 30 feet.. The tediously slow advance of the Allied forces on Buna Mission likewise in large measure was attributable to the ingenunity with which Japanese bunkers and machine gun emplacements were camouflaged. In contrast, however, there have been many instances where camouflage was hasty and slip-shod, or little effort was made to hide installations from aerial observation.

A most common Japanese method of camouflage utilizes natural cover and local vegetation, supplemented by artificial means only when necessary. Effective natural camouflage conforms in size and texture to the surroundings, and does not present a peculiar appearance.

On Makin Island the Japanese depended mainly upon the thick natural cover of coconut trees and other vegetation. This cover, used frequently in combination with transplantings, was employed to camouflage virtually all defensive installations. For example, the defenders constructed a concrete pillbox under the fronds of a small palm tree, and placed turf on top

Figure 35.—Camouflaged gun position (Gilbert Islands).

of the structure and small pandamus trees around it. Log pillboxes were covered with dirt, rocks, and short pieces of logs, and further concealed by shrubs and saplings implanted in a realistic manner.

The same method was used in concealing beach defenses. Rifle pits and machine-gun emplacements were constructed directly behind the beach under the fringe of coconut trees along the shore, and the low undergrowth in front of the positions was left intact.

Some of the buildings were constructed with large breadfruit trees growing within them. The trees were not a part of the structure of the buildings, but were pruned, when necessary, so that their growth would continue unhampered.

The Japanese frequently have used live grass, or other live vegetation which is either sown or transplanted, to cover their pillboxes, bunkers, and dugouts. Turf is used mainly on earth works. It is placed on the required surface so that it resembles natural grass in every respect. Only the turf taken from the earth where the position is located, or grass of the same variety, density, shape, and height of the grass growing around the installation is used. Sandbags, which ordinarily would be placed on top of pillboxes or other installations, have sometimes been replaced by rice-straw bags filled with fertile dirt and planted on top with rice seeds, or seeds of a similar plant, to secure a green growth to blend with the surroundings. Vines and brush are allowed to grow over concrete pillboxes.

The Japanese also use cut palm fronds for camouflage. These are placed on the roofs of buildings to conceal them and to protect the corrugated iron roofs from direct rays of the sun. Fronds also are placed on roofs of small buildings, either to conceal them from air observation or

Figure 36.—Camouflaged 8-inch battery on Betio.

Figure 37.—Japanese 3-inch gun well camouflaged on a Saipan beach.

to make them resemble native structures. Open emplacements for coast defense guns frequently may have palm-frond canopies over them.

Palm fronds are spread over movable stores or new installations so that the covering blends with the surroundings. A torpedo repair shop on Guam was located beneath palm trees. The repaired torpedoes also were covered with palm fronds. Similar camouflage was used instead of camouflage nets to cover the loose stores, which included all types of military equipment, such as drums of gasoline and oil, airplane motors, chemical warfare equipment, airplane gas tanks, demolition equipment and ammunition boxes.

The Japanese use nets extensively, particularly in jungle areas, to conceal not only personnel but weapons and installations as well. The artillery net is large enough to cover a gun and its crew. Nets are made of greenish-colored straw, fiber, wire, cord, or ordinary twine, with the square mesh slightly under two inches in size. String nets are dipped in astringent dyes, and wire is smoked in a straw fire to remove its shine and make it more pliable.

Nets are arranged to conform to the contour of the land. Care is taken to avoid gaps between sections. Nets are installed so that they slope gently where they touch the ground, with frames as low as possible. To avoid casting shadows under nets, canvases are set up under them. Branches, leaves, grass, and other local vegetation usually are stuck into the nets so as to blend with surroundings. Grass is sometimes hung on wire to disguise the terrain as a grass thicket.

Peepholes and loopholes, when the latter are not in use, may be covered with nets, or concealed with grass.

Screens are used for concealment against ground reconnaissance and to cut off the flash of weapons at night. They are made of light material such as bamboo, and covered with grass and nets. There are two types of screens, portable and stationary. Stationary screens may be made large enough to cover a position.

When paint is used to make an object blend with the terrain, the principal colors should approximate the predominant colors of the terrain, or be somewhat darker. Paint thus is used in connection with natural cover. Concrete pillboxes on Guam had been colored while the concrete was still wet. Then, vines and brush were allowed to grow over them.

On Makin, deceptive painting, in various tones of red and gray, was used on the roofs of some buildings to make them blend into the foliage. Many buildings, constructed by the British before the Japanese occupation, were disruptively painted in this manner. Strips of greatly varying width were usually painted roughly parallel to the length of the building. In cases where this type of painting was used, no palm fronds were placed on roofs of the building. All of the heavy guns on Makin were disruptively painted red, yellow, green, and blue.

Except for the use of sod to cover revetments, the Japanese until recent months made little effort to conceal antiaircraft positions. However, they are now utilizing palm-frond canopies quite extensively in camouflaging open emplacements, and rope netting also is used to some extent. Several antiaircraft batteries at Vila were emplaced in coconut groves, with apparently little regard for firing obstructions.

Dummy installations are employed by the Japanese to create an illusion of strength and to draw fire to areas where little damage will result to their real positions. Those on Saipan, Guam, and Makin were well constructed and located in logical positions; in some cases they were effective in deceiving photo interpreters and forward artillery spotters. Details of installations on Saipan were especially noteworthy. Searchlights were accurate in detail and complete even to dummy figures of crews. Nearby was a dummy defense gun and range finder to further the illusion of a profitable target.

Figure 38.—Dummy range finder on Saipan.

Installations were made to resemble coast defense guns with shields, single-mount antiaircraft guns, and twin- and triple-mount large caliber machine guns. Camouflage dazzle paint was used to avoid an unnatural appearance, and white stones leading from gun positions to range finder and observation posts indicated track activities.

Dummy installations on Guam followed the same pattern as those on Saipan. A simulated coast defense gun on the west end of Cabras Island was placed on a concrete base built by U. S. forces for a real gun emplacement.

Dummy installations on Makin were built of material available on the spot. Coconut logs, burlap, and, in some instances, coral were used to create the effect of coast defense antiaircraft guns. Those constructed on

Figure 39.—Dummy antiaircraft gun.

the west coast were placed to "guard" the best stretch of landing beach on that side of the island, and purposely were made discernible by aerial photograph. They were built in coral-stone revetments or placed in posi-

Figure 40.—Dummy coast-defense gun.

tions constructed of coconut logs, and projected from 1 to 3½ feet out of the ground.

Airfields

General Description

Many of the islands thus far invaded by U. S. forces had been occupied by the Japanese primarily to extend their network of air bases. In some cases the islands had little or no value other than to afford strategic sites for the construction of airdromes, and defensive installations were laid out to provide last-ditch protection for the landing strips.

The Japanese have constructed or taken over a surprisingly large number of airfields. In the Philippines, for example, as of August, 1944, there were 270 identified airfields, 18 of which were all-weather fields equipped to handle any type of plane, while 115 were landing grounds without all-weather runways or completely adequate facilities. One hundred twenty seven were emergency fields, and 10 were seaplane bases. In Burma, French Indo-China, Malaya, and Thailand, at about the same time, there was a total of 527 identified fields, and in the Japanese Islands proper, 471.

The large number of fields already built, as well as the number under construction, indicates that the Japanese plan a wide dispersal of their air power and extensive shifting of strength over the tremendous areas in which they must provide air coverage against the staggering air and naval power of the allies.

Airfields have been built, obviously, for general strategic and tactical purposes. Yet when they are located near defended beaches, they naturally are integrated with the general plan for coast defense. Patrol planes are based on them for long-range reconnaissance, and heavy bombers strike from them at hostile naval forces far at sea. Fighters and medium bombers are assigned important roles in frustrating enemy landing attempts and airborne attacks.

The type of airfield which the Japanese construct on an island is contingent upon the shape and size of the island. Long, narrow islands usually have but one strip. On circular islands, two criss-crossed strips normally are built, whereas on crescent-shaped islands a triangle of three strips often is laid out.

Concrete frequently is used to surface runways intended to accommodate the heavier planes in all types of weather. Asphalt, bitumen mixed with coral sand, crushed rock and earth, and sod also are used, depending upon the importance and purpose of the field and the materials available. Turn-arounds usually are constructed at each end of the landing strips which are oriented to take advantage of the direction of prevailing winds.

Dispersal areas are provided with an adequate number of well-built revetments for the protection of planes against aerial bombing and artillery bombardment. On Munda, for example, such revetments were constructed with coconut logs, coral, or a combination of both. They were 7 to 10 feet high, and their size was in proportion to the type of planes they were intended to protect. Ordinarily, revetments for fighter planes were square, about 45 feet on a side. Those for bombers were rectangular, with dimensions approximately 95 feet by 90 feet. Reports from other areas indicate that small railway cars loaded with logs and sandbags occasionally have been pushed in front of the revetments to act as blast walls during aerial attacks.

When hangars are built they usually are located right on the service aprons and are conventional in design. There is evidence that underground hangars have been constructed in some areas. In China, Thailand, and Burma, so-called hangarettes have been observed. These are wood or light bamboo frames covered with open-work matting.

Both two- and three-dimensional dummy aircraft, as well as unserviceable planes and dummy corner markers, often are used for deception. Camouflage, while usually adequate to make identification of the types of planes difficult, often is ineffective in masking the presence of the aircraft.

Typical Fields

Description of several typical airfields may be taken as representative of the principles that govern Japanese construction. The airdrome on Peleliu was considered the major base in the Western Carolines. It had two concrete-surfaced runways, in criss-cross patterns, one 3,990 feet long and the other 3,850 feet, centered in a clearing approximately 5,000 by 2,000 feet. There were extensive dispersal areas, and turning circles, 460 feet in diameter, at the ends of each runway. In addition to hangars and a control tower, installations included buildings for major repairs, two radio stations, and 2 radar assemblies. More than a score of automatic antiaircraft guns protected the field.

The Aslito field on Saipan had a hard-surfaced runway, 3,600 feet long and 900 feet wide, and a diagonal runway of the same width was under construction. The Marpi Point field, also on Saipan, had a runway 4,400 by 210 feet, and was equipped with underground storage facilities and revetments which were built close to a hillside so as to provide additional protection from aerial attack. The Tinian field had a runway 4,750 by 275 feet, larger than those on Saipan or Truk. Guam, which was not fortified with the same thoroughness as Saipan and Tinian, had three airfields. One at Orote had asphalt-coral surfacing and was 5,400 by 320 feet. Two others were in process of construction at the time of the U. S. invasion.

The San Rogue field in Southwest Mindanao has a runway oriented ESE—NNW. Hard-surfaced, it is 6,600 by 325 feet, and is adequate to accommodate all types of planes. Surrounding ground areas are level and well drained. The north taxi loop is 12,000 by 100 feet, while a similar one on the south is 10,000 by 75 feet. There are 18 revetments, 9 at the north taxi loop and the same number at the south. Each revetment measures about 80 by 60 feet, and there are a total of 200 hardstands for bombers and fighters. Servicing is apparently done on the taxiways. Buildings include a 30 by 80 feet workshop, and a 40 by 240 feet warehouse. The fiield is defended by 6 medium and 8 light antiaircraft guns.

Chapter IV

Japanese Coast Defense Guns

A considerable variety of coast defense guns have been mounted in Japanese installations encountered to date. Most of these were naval guns, which in many cases have been removed along with their turrets and mountings from the decks of warships. Others were guns of naval design, adapted for coast defense use; a considerable number were British weapons.

8-Inch Guns

On Betio island (Tarawa), two Armstrong-Whitworth Model 1905 8-inch, coast defense guns, 45 calibers long, were found mounted in a tandem arrangement. They were mounted on pedestals set in concrete, in a

Figure 41.—Left side of 8-inch gun emplacement on Betio.

circular emplacement, 38 to 40 feet in diameter, revetted with concrete, and banked with sand.

The weapon has a barrel 30 feet long, extending 19.2 feet from the front of the steel shield to the muzzle. Its rifling is peculiar. One-fifth of the barrel length, looking forward from the breech, has straight rifling, which changes to a clockwise twist for the remaining length to the muzzle. One gun of the tandem had a 270-degree traverse, while the other had a full 360 degrees. Maximum elevation has been reported to be 30 degrees. The maximum range has been estimated at 19,000 to 25,000 yards.

The guns fire armor-piercing shells weighing about 254 pounds, with a 2.5-inch penetration at 5,000 yards at a 90-degree angle of impact. Training and pointing of the guns were by electrical apparatus located beneath the surface of the concrete gun deck. Here, too, were located the air flasks which furnished a blast to clear the bore of the guns after firing.

Figure 42.—8-inch gun emplacement on southwest point of Betio island. Note camouflage and sand-banked concrete revetment.

The shield of each piece was rounded in front and extended to the rear so as to cover the breech. The forward armor was 2¼ inches thick, while at the sides it was 1 inch. Evidence of the effectiveness of the armor was the fact that it withstood a direct hit by a 5-inch naval shell.

A steel ammunition trough, 2 feet high and 8 inches wide, almost completely surrounded the guns. Ammunition was stored in a heavily constructed bomb-proof shelter 75 yards from the gun position. From here, a narrow-gauge railroad led to the ammunition ready-room located between the two guns. Ammunition was loaded on small hand-drawn cars and brought to the ready-room, which was constructed of reinforced concrete 30 inches thick. Here the ammunition was lifted to the trough partially encircling the guns by a chain hoist. From the trough, a davit-type crane on the gun mount lifted the shells into the loading tray from which they were shoved into the breech by a folding movable tray.

A crew of 63 manned the two guns, together with 12 additional men who served as ammunition passers. Fire-control equipment included a plotting room in the lower level of the upper gun emplacement. An observation tower, 70 feet in height, was built over a concrete platform to house the range finder and locator.

Figure 43.—Looking from lower to upper piece of 8-inch gun tandem emplacement on Betio.

On the southeast coast, two guns of this type were located in concrete emplacements which raised them 10 feet above the ground level. The guns had the same characteristics as those described above, except that they each had a 300-degree traverse. Ammunition, powder, and crew were sheltered in four concrete magazines. A fire-control tower, 45 feet high and located behind the guns, mounted a range finder.

An 8-inch British Armstrong-Whitworth gun, not a 1905 Model, also is in use by the Japanese. It is 40 calibers in length, and fires a 254-pound projectile that will penetrate 2.5-inch armor at 20,000 yards. Its muzzle velocity is 2,600 feet per second, and its maximum range on ship mount is estimated at 21,000 yards. The gun has a traverse of 360 degrees, and, on ship mount, a maximum elevation of 35 degrees. A Russian-made 8-inch gun, 45 calibers long, likewise has been emplaced in Japanese coastal defense installations.

A Japanese 8-inch (20-cm) short naval gun was found emplaced on both Saipan and Peleliu. Referred to in a Japanese naval gunnery manual as experimental, the weapon apparently was designed for use on merchant ships over 5,000 tons for antiaircraft and antisubmarine purposes.

The bore, which is 203.2-mm, extends for 7 feet, 11 inches. The gun, which with its mount weighs 6 tons, has an elevation of 65 degrees and a depression of minus 15 degrees. It must be brought to an elevation of 15 degrees for loading.

Muzzle velocity is 1,000 feet per second with a shell weighing 103.62 pounds. The gun has a range of 6,900 yards, or a vertical range of 10,750 feet when used as an antiaircraft weapon. Rate of fire is 5½ rounds per minute at low elevation and 4 rounds per minute at high elevation when the weapon is served by its full crew of 9.

6-Inch Guns

On Kiska, a three-gun battery of 6-inch (152.4-mm) naval guns was found in revetments, 26 to 30 feet in diameter. This gun has an over-all length of 20 feet, and is 12 feet from the wedge-shaped shield to the muzzle. It has a traverse of 360 degrees and an elevation of approximately 30 degrees. The breech is of the interrupted screw type. The shield is 1¼ inches thick on the sides and has a 4-inch plate in front. Ammunition is of the semifixed type, and the powder charge is one increment. Separate primers are used which are screwed into the cartridge case after a plug placed in the hole for shipping is removed.

A battery of two similar Armstrong-Whitworth 6-inch naval guns was emplaced at Agingan Point, Saipan. One was sited to fire on the channel between Tinian and Saipan, while the other commanded the approaches to beaches. One gun was in a completed concrete casemate, but a similar casemate for the other had not been finished before U. S. forces captured the island. The casemates limited the traverse of each weapon to 90 degrees, and ammunition storage facilities also were restricted, since only 100 rounds were stored in a cave 600 yards southeast of the gun position.

A battery of four of these guns was located on Nafutan Point; three were in open circular emplacements, 35 feet in diameter, with walls and parapets 30 inches high. The fourth gun was set up in a partially completed reinforced concrete emplacement. All these weapons were emplaced to allow a 180-degree traverse, and each gun had a protected ammunition magazine for 48 rounds. Another battery of two guns was sited to fire on Tanapag harbor. One gun was in an open emplacement; the other was in an incomplete concrete casemate.

Other specimens of 6-inch naval guns doubtless will be encountered. This type of 6-inch naval gun is 40 calibers long and fires a 100-pound projectile that penetrates 2.6 inches of armor at 15,000 yards. Its muzzle velocity is 2,800 feet per second, and its maximum range 14,000 yards.

Figure 44.—Views of 8-inch short naval gun. This weapon has been encountered on Saipan and at Peleliu.

Figure 45.—Views of 6-inch 40 caliber coast defense gun with shield.

Figure 46.—Armstrong-Whitworth Model 1900 6-inch naval gun.

Figure 47.—A Japanese 6-inch gun emplaced on Chonito Cliff, Guam.

Figure 48.—Two views of the 1912 Model 15-cm gun.

Elevation, on the older type of ship mounts, is 20 degrees, and traverse 360 degrees.

The Battleship Kongo class 6-inch naval gun allegedly is 50 calibers long, and fires a 150-pound projectile that penetrates 2.2 inches of armor at 15,000 yards. Its muzzle velocity is only 2,300 feet per second, but its maximum range is 18,000 yards. Elevation and traverse are 20 and 360 degrees, respectively. Mention also should be made of the Schneider 155-mm naval gun, which is 50 calibers in length and fires a 123.5-pound projectile at a muzzle velocity of 2,854 feet per second.

14-cm and 12-cm Guns

Four 14-cm Model 3 (1914) naval guns were found on Betio, two on the northwest point, and two on the east point. These shield-covered

Figure 49.—Views of 14-cm naval gun emplaced in turret on Betio with shields of type used on Nigara class cruisers.

Figure 50.—Japanese 14-cm naval gun with battleship casemate type of shield at Enogai Inlet, New Georgia (above); rear view of 14-cm naval gun (below).

coast defense guns were mounted in circular concrete pits with diameters of 35 to 38 feet. The two emplacements were about 60 yards apart in each area, and were at normal ground level.

The gun is 23 feet 8 inches long and is rifled for 19 feet 3½ inches. There are 42 lands and grooves, with the bore from land to land 5.512 inches and from groove to groove 5.614 inches. The chamber is 43 inches long and the breechblock 9½ inches. The breechblock is three-threaded, with two-step segments, and the recoil mechanism is hydropneumatic.

Pointers and trainers are located on the gun mount, and the weapon is believed to be elevated and trained by hand. The traverse is 360 degrees, and the elevation from minus 7 to plus 30 degrees. Muzzle velocity, according to the range disk, is 2,830 feet per second, giving a maximum range of 19,000 yards.

The cruiser-type shield, with rounded corners, has armor 1.5 inches thick on the sides and 0.5 inch on top. The mantlet is 1 inch thick. In the Betio installations, ammunition was moved to the guns from the magazines on hand-cars running on a narrow gauge railroad laid in a trench. Nine men constituted the actual crew of a gun, and the total personnel assigned to the servicing of a pair of guns was 59.

Fire was controlled on Betio from an observation tower 80 feet high, built on top of a concrete, sand covered, bomb-proof shelter. Inside the shelter was located a power distribution board for the supply of electricity to the battery, as well as a communication center.

Figure 51.—14-cm naval gun at Enogai Inlet, New Georgia, in open emplacement.

The 12-cm (120-mm) Third Year Type coastal gun apparently was designed for mounting on destroyers, for four of them were found on an old-type destroyer beached off Kolombangara. On Baanga Island, guns of this type were found mounted in covered dugouts which limited their normal 360-degree traverse to 70 degrees.

Total length of the gun is 18 feet, 4 inches; it is 6 feet, 5½ inches wide, and 12 feet, 5 inches high at maximum elevation and 6 feet at maximum depression. Elevation is 33 degrees, and the maximum depression is minus 7 degrees. According to the range scale, the muzzle velocity with full charge is 2,679 feet per second and the maximum range 16,350 yards.

The rifling, which is of the uniform right-hand type, extends for 15 feet, 7½ inches of the barrel length. The chamber is 21½ inches long. Bore is 4.737 inches from land to land, and 4.797 inches from groove to groove; there are 36 lands and grooves. The breech is the two-step, horizontal, swinging, interrupted-screw type. There are no equilibrators, and the recoil mechanism is believed to be hydropneumatic. Ammunition is separate loading with cartridge case. The only type thus far found is nose-fuzed HE with a short radius of ogive and a flat base.

No exterior fire control equipment has been found. Firing normally is conducted by direct sighting through a telescopic sight and the use of range scales.

4.7-Inch Guns

A gun of British manufacture, which also has been produced in Japan, is the Model 1905 4.7-inch (120-mm) coast defense gun. On Kiska, four of these guns were emplaced, two of which were made by Armstrong-Whitworth, while the others were manufactured at the Kure Naval Arsenal. All were mounted on pedestals set in concrete and emplaced in circular revetments. The emplacements had an inside diameter of about 20 feet and were spaced at approximately 55-feet intervals.

The weapon, which has a barrel 16.5 feet long, is not equipped with a shield. Its traverse is 360 degrees, and elevation is 30 degrees. The breech is of the interrupted-screw type. Ammunition is semifixed, with one increment of powder. The gun is fired by an electric trigger, the mechanism of which is controlled by the gunner. On Kiska, a telephone and buzzer installation connected the gun positions with a fire control center equipped with a 3-meter range finder. Two 150-cm searchlights were located near the battery.

An experimental short 4.7-inch (120-mm) naval gun is described in a Japanese naval gunnery manual, but no specimens as yet have been recovered. The barrel is rifled for 4 feet, 8.7 inches. Elevation of the weapon is 75 degrees and depression minus 15 degrees. The gun can be loaded at any elevation less than 20 degrees. It fires a shell weighing 28.66 pounds at a muzzle velocity of 950 feet per second. The maximum ranges are 5,775 yards horizontal and 9,100 feet vertical. Served by a crew of

Figure 52 (a).—The 12-cm (120-mm) Model 3 naval gun.

Figure 52 (b).—Another view of the 120-mm Model 3 naval gun.

7, the gun can fire 12 rounds per minute at low elevation and 7 rounds per minute at high elevation.

8-cm and 75-mm Guns

One of the most widely employed Japanese coastal guns found in the combat theaters to date is the 8-cm (76-mm) Vickers Type weapon. Two-thirds of them thus far encountered have been of actual Vickers manufacture. A Japanese copy has been produced, however, identical with the original model except for minor changes in the recoil cylinder, the sight mount and sight mount bracket, and the design of the cradle. The Japanese pieces probably were made at the Sasebo Naval Arsenal, and it is believed that they originally were mounted on destroyers.

Two pieces of British manufacture were installed at Kolombangara, and they also have been found on New Georgia. On Betio, two batteries of three guns each were found—one in the center of the west beach, the other on the eastern part of the south shore where it had the mission of covering the south reef antitank barrier with flanking fire. Emplacements were of log and sand construction, open at the top except for palm-branch camouflage. They were hexagonal in shape, with the entrance at the rear, and the gun pedestals rested on concrete bases. Walls of the emplacements consisted of two rows of logs laid horizontally to a height of about 3 feet. Space between the rows was filled with sand. The front side of the emplacements were parallel to the beach. Ammunition shelters were built into the rear walls, each capable of holding three ammunition boxes of 12-round capacity.

Bomb-proof shelters, each adequate to hold 12 men, were located to the rear and to one side of each emplacement. A log observation tower, 10 by 10 feet at its base and 15 feet high, stood just behind and a little to one side of the central gun of each battery.

Besides the normal hexagonal open emplacement on Kiska, two covered emplacements were found in the cliff overlooking a strategic harbor area. These covered positions were about 16 feet square and were covered with sand, earth, or coral and logs.

The over-all length of the gun and its mount is 11 feet, 3 inches; the gun alone is 10 feet long. Rifling of the tube is uniform right hand with 24 lands, extending for 8 feet, $3\frac{1}{3}$ inches. The bore is 3.005 inches from land to land and 3.050 inches from groove to groove. The chamber is 1 foot, $6\frac{1}{2}$ inches long. The recoil system is of the hydrospring type. The gun is mounted at the point of balance, and consequently there are no equilibrators.

Traverse of the weapon is 360 degrees; elevation is 20 degrees and depressions minus 5 degrees. In view of its limited elevation, the weapon cannot be used for antiaircraft fire. The range scale discs found with the guns give the range as 8,700 yards with Type 3 "standard" ammunition and 6,600 yards with Type 3 "ordinary". Muzzle velocity with the Type 3

Figure 53.—Views of Model 3 (1914) 12-cm naval gun with destroyer-type of shield.

"standard", which apparently gives the maximum range (8,700 yards), is stated to be 2,260 feet per second.

Ammunition is semifixed loading with a propelling charge contained in the cartridge case. The only type found for guns emplaced as coast defense weapons is a nose-fuzed HE round. The projectile is flat-based, with a one-piece rotating band and a short radius of ogive. The projectile is dull red with dark green rings around the nose. The propelling charge is single perforated spaghetti type, while the primer igniter is conventional—a percussion type which screws into the base of the cartridge case with a standard right-hand thread.

Four Model 30 (1897) 8-cm naval guns were found covering a vital harbor area on Kiska. It is probable that they had been removed from Japanese ships beached in the harbor. The gun bases were mounted in concrete in covered revetments 13 feet square. Although the guns have a traverse of 360 degrees, the covered revetments greatly limited this, and there was no elevation, although normally the guns are capable of a 30-degree elevation.

Guns of this type have a barrel 10 feet long. The breech is of the interrupted screw type. Ammunition is semi-fixed, with a single-increment powder charge. There was no shield for the weapons found on Kiska.

Two old Model 38 (1905) 75-mm converted field guns also constituted part of the Kiska defense armament. They were installed in circular revetments with respective diameters of 12 and 14 feet, and each gun was mounted on a pedestal set in concrete. The barrels were mounted on the original unimproved type of cradle with hydro-spring recoil mechanism. Both weapons had a traverse of 360 degrees, and an elevation of approximately 40 degrees. The breechblocks were of the sliding-wedge type. Each gun was equipped with a detachable shield of ½-inch steel plate which provided only frontal protection.

Heavy Guns Not Yet Encountered

Besides pieces already encountered, a number of heavier naval guns are known to have been emplaced in various Japanese coast defense installations. The Model 1893 270-mm (10.6-inch) Schneider gun, a weapon 45 calibers long, fires an armor-piercing projectile weighing 579.1 pounds. Its muzzle velocity is about 2,600 feet per second, and its maximum range approximately 26,000 yards. As in the case of other naval guns, maximum range figures apply to the guns when mounted on warships and naturally would be affected by the character of such land mounts as might be utilized. Elevation and traverse are limited by ship structure, whereas in coast defense emplacements these characteristics would be subject to conditions imposed by the terrain and the nature of the emplacements.

A 270-mm Schneider gun, 45 calibers long and manufactured in the period 1893–1896, also is known to be emplaced in Japanese coast defense positions. It fires an armor-piercing shell weighing 580 pounds, at a muzzle

Figure 54.—24-cm gun (above); 28-cm howitzer (below).

velocity of 2,700 feet per second with a maximum range, on ship mount, of 20,000 yards. For naval use the gun has a maximum elevation of 25 degrees.

Ten-inch weapons known to be utilized for coastal defense include a Russian 10-inch naval gun which is 45 calibers long and fires a projectile that penetrates 9.75 inches of armor at 5,000 yards. An Armstrong-Whitworth 10-inch weapon of the same caliber also may be encountered. It fires a projectile having a ¾ of an inch greater penetration at 5,000 yards than the Russian gun.

A 10.8-inch gun of unknown manufacture has been described as a weapon 45 calibers in length with a maximum range of 24,000 yards. A British 9.2-inch coast-defense gun 45 calibers long also is used; it fires a 380-pound projectile. This latter weapon has an elevation of 35 degrees, an estimated maximum range, with a supercharge of 31,300 yards and a muzzle velocity of 2,825 feet per second.

Figure 55.—6-inch 40 caliber coast defense gun encountered on Guam.

Two 12-inch guns are known to be in use, one manufactured by the Japanese, the other of English make. The Japanese weapon is 45 calibers long and fires a projectile that will pierce 16-inch armor at 5,000 yards. The English gun, 40 calibers in length, fires a 1,400-pound armor-piercing projectile, with a penetration of 6.5 inches at 30,000 yards. The muzzle velocity of this weapon is 2,600 feet per second, and its maximum range is 32,000 yards. Its maximum elevation on ship mount is 35 degrees, and it can be traversed 360 degrees.

Another coast defense gun that has been identified is the 14-inch, 40-calibers-in-length naval gun of the battleships of the Kongo class. It fires a 1,400-pound projectile that pentrates 6.5 inches of armor at 30,000 yards. Its muzzle velocity is 2,600 feet per second, and maximum range is 32,000 yards. Traverse of the weapon is 360 degrees, and elevation 35 degrees on naval mounting.

A 16-inch gun of the Nagato class of battleships also has been installed in Japanese coast defense positions. This gun is 45 calibers long and fires a 2,200-pound armor-piercing projectile that will penetrate 10 inches at 30,000 yards. It has a 360-degree traverse and a maximum elevation of 35 degrees. Its maximum range, on ship mount, is estimated at 36,000 yards.

The Model 1929 240-mm railway gun also will be utilized by the Japanese. This gun has a bore 51 calibers in length. The muzzle velocity of the weapon has been reported at 3,560 feet per second, and, with an HE shell, the maximum range allegedly is 54,500 yards. Maximum elevation of the piece is 50 degrees, and total traverse 360 degrees. The weight of the piece ready for action is approximately 35 tons.

Figure 56.—24-cm gun, Schneider, railway mount.

Field Artillery in Coast Defense

In a number of instances Japanese field artillery has been used in coastal defense roles. On Attu, field artillery batteries, armed with 75-mm guns, were boldly sited so that their fire could be concentrated on landing craft, and antipersonnel fire could be brought to bear on troops already disembarked. In the Marshall and Gilbert Islands, field guns were sited to lay flat-trajectory fire on landing boats and vehicles that had been put ashore. The guns were placed well forward for direct laying, but the positions were not in depth. Batteries had local fire control, with two or three guns usually controlled from observation towers at the gun positions.

On Saipan, on high ground and on a reverse slope 3,000 yards southeast of the beaches, were emplaced sixteen 105-mm howitzers and thirty 75-mm field pieces. Three thousand yards east of one of the beaches a four-gun battery of 150-mm howitzers was emplaced, with the pieces especially well sited. A battery of four 75-mm light mountain guns was emplaced practically on the beach, 1,000 yards southeast of the southern limits of Charan-Manoa and sited to fire on a channel through the reef through which landing boats had to pass. In all, thirty-nine 75-mm, eight 105-mm, and twelve 150-mm pieces were found on the island.

Eighteen Model 95 (1935) 75-mm field guns were captured. This weapon has an estimated maximum range with pointed shell of about 12,000 yards. Its tube is 89.7 inches long. Total traverse is 50 degrees; elevation is 43 degrees and depression minus 8 degrees. The breech is of the horizontal sliding-wedge type, and the recoil system is hydropneumatic.

The Model 94 (1934) 75-mm mountain gun employed by the Japanese on Kiska and Saipan has replaced the earlier Model 41 (1908) 75-mm weapon as the standard weapon of Japanese pack artillery. It has hydropneumatic recoil, continuous-pull percussion firing mechanism, a horizontal sliding-wedge breech, pintle traverse, three-point suspension, and split trails which are equipped with spade plates as stabilizers. The gun can be animal packed or hand carried, and it is reported that it can be disassembled in about 5 minutes and reassembled in approximately twice that time. The tube is 61.5 inches in length. Traverse totals 40 degrees; elevation is 45 degrees, and depression minus 10 degrees. It is reported, however, that the counter-recoil is very slow when the piece is fired at elevations greater than 30 degrees. The maximum range with pointed shell is about 8,900 yards, and 8,000 yards with HE.

The Model 91 (1931) 10-cm (105-mm) howitzer is a standard Japanese field artillery piece that has been employed in coast defense. It is of extremely light construction in relation to its range and the weight of its projectile. Its split trail has demountable spade plates, and another prominent identification characteristic is the long cradle which extends almost to the muzzle of the tube. The tube is 8 feet 4 inches in length, while the over-all length of the piece in firing position is 15 feet, 6 inches. It is horse-drawn, and in traveling position is 29 feet, 4 inches long and weighs 4,364 pounds.

The pintle traverse permits a total turning of 40 degrees; elevation is 45 degrees, and depression minus 5 degrees. Maximum range with the heaviest charge used is about 11,775 yards. The breachblock is of the interrupted-screw type, and a percussion hammer firing mechanism is employed. The recoil system is hydropneumatic.

The Model 4 (1915) 150-mm howitzer which has been encountered in coastal defense installations has a barrel 85.4 inches long. The gun is extremely light for a weapon of this caliber, and it breaks down into two loads for horse-drawn transport. This weapon is the first Japanese piece to employ a hydropneumatic recoil system, and its modified box trail allows it to fire at the unusual elevation of 65 degrees. It can be depressed to minus 5 degrees, and the total traverse is 6 degrees. Range is about 10,000 yards, with a muzzle velocity of 1,345 feet per second.

On Betio, Model 41 (1908) 75-mm cavalry guns as well as the 70-mm howitzer were used in coast defense roles. These guns were used as antiboat weapons and in support of major defense positions. Emplacements were either arrow- or egg-shaped, with the gun in the open end. Walls of the emplacements were formed by a single layer of logs lashed to retaining sticks or joined at the corners with steel-rod staples and banked on the outside with loose sand. All positions had unroofed entrance passageways in the rear, usually 5 to 10 feet long and 5 to 6 feet wide. In a few instances, these passageways were straight; more commonly, however, they curved in order to provide blast protection. All firing ports were sealed and sheltered from blast and small-arms fire by log- and sand-banked wings, 5 to 8 feet long and opening to an angle of approximately 100 degrees.

It is quite likely that the Model 45 (1912) 240-mm howitzer will be encountered in emplacement for coast defense. This piece allegedly can be disassembled into units which are transported in 10 vehicles. It fires a semifixed round weighing approximately 400 pounds, and its maximum range is reputed to be about 11,000 yards.

Guns Captured by the Japanese

Any discussion of Japanese coastal artillery resources must take into serious consideration the large number of heavy caliber weapons which fell into Japanese hands with the conquests of the Philippines, Hong Kong, and Singapore. According to available information the following tables represent an appraisal of U. S. and British coast defense guns which are integral parts of present Japanese defenses:

COAST DEFENSE GUNS IN THE PHILIPPINES

	Armament			Nomenclature		Remarks
No.	Cal.	Type	Gun	Carriage		

	No.	Cal.	Type	Gun	Carriage	Remarks
Fort Mills—Corregidor batteries:						
Cheney	2	12"	DC	M1895M1	M1901DC	
Crockett	2	12"	DC	M1895M1	M1901DC	
Hearn	1	12" LR	BC	M1895M1A2	M1917BC	(1)
Smith	1	12"	BC	M1895M1A3	M1917BC	
Wheeler	2	12"	DC	M1895M1	M1901DC	(1)
Geary Pit "A"	4	12"	Mortars	M1890	M1896M1	(1)
Geary Pit "B"	4	12"	Mortars	M1908	M1896M1	(1)
Way	4	12"	Mortars	M1890M1	M1896M1	
Grubbs	2	10"	DC	M1895M1	M1901DC	(1)
Morison	2	6"	DC	M1905	M1905M1DC	(1)
Ramsey	3	6"	DC	M1905	M1905DC	(1)
Cushing	2	3"	Ped BC	M1903	M1903	
Hanna	1	3"	Ped BC	M1903	M1903	
Hanna	1	3"	BC	M1903	M1903	
James	4	3"	Ped BC	M1903	M1903	
Maxwell Keyes	2	3"	Ped BC	M1903	M1903	
Sunset	4	155 mm				(2)
Conception	2	155 mm				
Monja	2	155 mm				(3)
North	2	155 mm				
Ord Point B, 92 CA	2	155 mm				
Ord Point C, 92 CA	2	155 mm				
Rock Point	2	155 mm				
South	2	155 mm				(4)
Stockade	2	155 mm				
AA Battery #4	2	3"	AA			
AA Battery #2	5	3"	AA			
AA Battery #5	1	3"	AA			

88

Fort Wint—Grande					
Warwick	2	10″	DC	M1895M1	M1901DC	(5)
Hall	2	6″	DC	M1905	M1905DC	
Woodruff	2	6″	DC	M1905	M1905DC	
Flake	2	3″	BC	M1903	M1903	
Jewell	2	3″	BC	M1903	M1903	
AA Battery #1	2	3″	AA			
Subic	2	155 mm				
Fort Frank—Carabao						
Crofton	1	14″	DC	M1907M1	M1907DC	
Greer	1	14″	DC	M1907M1	M1907DC	
Kochler Pit "A"	4	12″	Mortars	M1908	M1908	
Kochler Pit "B"	4	12″	Mortars	M1908	M1908	
Frank North	2	155 mm		On Panama mounts		(3)
Frank South	2	155 mm		On Panama mounts		(6)
Hoyle	1	3″	BC	M1903	M1903	(1)
AA No. 8	4	3″	AA			(6)
Fort Hughes—Caballo						
Gillespie	1	14″	DC	M1910	M1907M1DC	
Woodruff	1	14″	DC	M1910	M1907M1DC	
Craighill	4	12″	Mortars	M1912	M1896M3	
Leach	2	6″	DC	M1908	M1905DC	
Hughes	1	155 mm				
Fuger	2	3″	BC	M1903	M1903	
AA No. 5	4	3″	AA			
Fort Drum—El Fraile						
Marshall	2	14″	Turret	M1909	Turret 1909	
Wilson	2	14″	Turret	M1909	Turret 1909	
McCrea	2	6″	BC	M1908M2	M1910BC	(7)
South Roberts	2	6″	BC	M1908M2	M1910BC	(7)
AA No. 7	2	3″	AA fixed	M1917 (fixed)	M1917 (fixed)	(6)

¹ 1 spare gun without carriage. ² Located 200 yds. N of Battery Smith; completed Oct. '41. Panama mounts. ³ 1 on casemate; 1 mobile on Panama mount. ⁴ On Panama mounts. ⁵ Fort Wint was evacuated by U. S. troops about 1 Jan. '42. The 155 battery was assigned to FA on Bataan. All fixed installations were probably demolished, not definitely known from reports at hand. ⁶ Reported destroyed. ⁷ Casemate.

A. Fixed Seacoast Artillery

No./spares	Item	Ammunition	Maximum range
2	Gun, 14'', M1907M1	M1909	*29,000
2	Carriage, 14'', D. C. M1907M1.ª		
2	Gun, 14'', M1910	M1909	*33,000
2	Carriage, 14'', D. C. M1907M1.		
4	Gun, 14'', M1909	Mk. VI	25,000
4	Turret Mount 14''.		
10/4	Gun, 12'', M1895M1	Mk. I	29,200
6	Carriage, 12'' D. C. M1901.		
1/1	Gun, 12'', M1895M1A3	Mk. X	30,000
2	Gun, 12'', M1895M1A2	Mk. VI	27,700
2	Carriage, B. C. M1917.ᵇ		
9/1	Mortar, 12'', M1890M1	M1898 & Mk. XXVIII	4,355
8	Carriage, Mortar, M1896M1.		
4	Mortar, 12'', M1912	Mk. XXVIII & M1898	4,825
4	Carriage, 12'' Mortar, M1896M3.		
12	Mortar, 12'', M1908	M1898 & Mk. XXVIII	7,115
12	Carriage, 12'' Mortar, M1908.		
5/1	Gun, 10'', D. C. M1895	Mk. III	17,000
4	Carriage, 10'', D. C. M1901.		
11	Gun, 6'', M1905	Mk. XXXIII, A. P.	27,150
2/2	Gun, 6'', M1908	M1911, A. P.	17,000
11	Carriage, 6'', D. C. M1905.		
4	Gun, 6'', M1908M2	Mk. II, H. E.	15,000
4	Carriage, 6'', B. C. M1910.		
24/7	Gun, 3'' (15 Pdr.), M1903	M42A1, H. E.	2,800
17	Carriage, 3'', B. C. (15 Pdr.), M1903.		
7(ᶜ)	Gun, 8'', M1888 (HD) (Ry. Guns for Fixed Emplacement).	Mk. VI	25,146
7(ᶜ)	Carriage, Barbette 8'', M1918.		

B. 155 mm (GPF) Guns (Mobile)

24	Gun, 155 mm, M1917A1	Mk. III, H. E.	17,900
41	Gun, 155 mm, M1918M1	Mk. III, H. E.	14,900
65	Carriages, 155 mm, M1918.		
?	Gun, 155 mm, M1A1	M101, H. E.	25,715

C. Antiaircraft Artillery

60	Gun, 3'', M3 on M3A2 Carriage (Mobile).	M42A1 (V. Range)	10,200
		APC M62A1 (H. Range)	16,100
2	Gun, 3'', M1917 & M1917M1 (Fixed on Mount M1917).	Mk. IX, H. E.	2,800
12	Gun, 3'', M1918 & M1918M1 on Mount M1918 & M1918M1.ᵈ	A. P. C. M62A1 (M-1918)	15,300
		M42A1, H. E. (M1918M1).	13,500(H) 9,420(V)
48	Gun, 37 mm, M3 on M3A1 & M3 Carriage.	M51B1, A. P. C.	12,850

*Estimated.
ª D. C.—Disappearing carriage.
ᵇ B. C.—Barbette carriage.
ᶜ Shipped to Philippines in early part of 1941 for use in fixed emplacements to cover the approaches to the Inland Seas formed by Luzon and the Visayan Islands. Twenty-four 155 mm guns in Philippines were also to be used for this project, but were later released to the Field Artillery.
ᵈ Intended for use in fixed positions.

D. Field Artillery Weapons

No./spares	Item	Ammunition	Maximum range
2	Howitzers, 155 mm, M1918	Mk. 1A1, H. E.	7,445
2	Carriages, How. 155 mm, M1918.		
14	Guns, 75 mm, M1916	Shell, H. E. Mk. I	8,865
	Carriages, Gun, 75 mm, M1916A1.		
208	Guns, 75 mm, M1917	Shell, H. E. Mk. I	8,865
81	Carriages, Gun, 75 mm, M1917.		
127	Carriages, Gun, 75 mm, M1917A1.		
72	Guns, 2.95″ Mtn	Shell, H. E. Mk. I	4,800
72	Carriages, Gun, 2.95″ Mtn.		
28	Guns, 75 mm, M1897A4 on Motor Carriages, T12.	A. P. M72	10,650

NOTE.—155 mm mobile guns, at least 24 of which were turned over to U. S. Field Artillery troops in the Philippine Islands, are listed in section B.

BRITISH COAST DEFENSE GUNS AT HONG KONG

	No.	Cal.	Mark
Hong Kong batteries.			
Stanley	3	9.2″	X.
Mt. Davis*	3	9.2″	X.
Bokhara*	2	9.2″	X.
Paksha Wan*	2	6″	VII.
Collinson	2	6″	VII.
Chung Am Kok	2	6″	VII.
Jubilee	3	6″	VII.
Stonecutters*	3	6″	VII.
Upper Belchers	1	6″	VII.
Lower Belchers	2	6″	VII (Naval).
Bluff Head	2	6″	VII (Naval).
Scandal Point	1	6″	VII.
(Reserve)	1	9.2″	X.
	2	6″	VII.
	20	8″ & 15″.	Barrels (Naval Guns).

*Confirmed by Photo Reconnaissance.

Additional guns and emplacements revealed by Photo Reconnaissance during March and April 1944.

Leiumun	2 unoccupied medium C/D positions.
Stanley Peninsula	60′ diameter revetments on SE tip and 1 heavy gun in 30′ revetment on SW tip (Bluff Head).
Ah Kung Ngam	2 gun positions.
Sai Wan Hill	2 new medium emplacements, unoccupied.
Tso Dai Wan	2 medium guns.
Hoinliung	2 light positions, 1 occupied.
West of Stanley POW Camp	3 medium emplacements 45′ in diameter under construction.
Chung Am Kok	1 possible 45′ emplacement unoccupied.
Mt. Parish	5 gun position, old permanent installation.
Scandal Point	5 gun probable dual-purpose battery, circular revetment 10′ in diameter. 4 gun probable A/A or dual purpose with adjacent revetment 15′ in diameter.
Mt. Davis	1 occupied medium or heavy C/D emplacement in concrete barbette 70′ in diameter. Similar emplacement probably occupied. 3 similar emplacements apparently occupied by guns of light caliber. 2 emplacements 45′ in diameter which appear unoccupied.
Sam Shui Kok	Revetment 15′ in diameter and West 2 C/D positions under construction and nearly completed.
West Pt. Apli Chau	2 C/D revetments under construction.

BRITISH COAST ARTILLERY PERFORMANCE DATA

Designation	M. V. f. s.	Max. depress., deg.	Max. range, yds.	Wt. of shell, lbs.	Wt. of charge, lbs.	Rate of fire, rpgpm*	Traverse, deg.	Remarks
15″ on Mk. I Mtg	2,400	5	36,900	1,938	432	1	240	Power operated.
15″ on Mk. II Mtg	2,400	2	36,900	1,938	432	2	240	
9.2″ on Mk. V Mtg	2,700	10	19,300	380	109 a	2	265	
9.2″ on Mk. VII Mtg b	2,700	5	29,600	380	109 a	3	360	
6″ Mk. VII:								
On Mk. II Mtg	2,525	10	14,100	100	23¼ SC	7	360	
On Mk. V Mtg	2,525	10	21,700	100	23¾ c	d 7	360	
On P. III Mtg	2,500	7	15,000	100	23¼	7	360	
6″ Mk. XI on P. III Mtg	2,900	7	14,500	100	33	7	360	

a Cordite SC 150. Supercharge SC 205 of 123¾ lbs. gives M. V. 2,825 and Max. Range 31,300 on Mk. VII Mtg.

b Power operated.

c Cordite W. 112. M. V. with charge W. 160 of 29 lbs. 14 oz. is 2,825 and Max. Range 24,500 on Mk. V Mtg.

d 4 at Max. Range.

*Rounds per gun per minute.

Chapter V
Dual-Purpose, Antiaircraft, and Machine Guns

Dual-Purpose and Antiaircraft Guns

The Japanese utilize dual-purpose guns in coast defense installations for antiboat and antipersonnel missions as well as for antiaircraft defense. One of the most effective of these weapons is the Model 10 (1921) 120-mm dual-purpose gun, four of which were emplaced as a battery on North Head, Kiska. The guns, probably manufactured in Japanese arsenals, were sited about 120 feet apart in revetments about 22 feet in diameter. A battery of four guns also was found southwest of Aslito airfield, on Saipan, in circular emplacements 5½ feet deep and approximately 22 feet in diameter. Here a precast concrete ammunition chamber, with a 60-round capacity, was provided for each gun.

Three guns were sited in somewhat smaller emplacements at the northeast point of the island, near the Marpi Point airfield. On a rocky point between two landing beaches, two others were located, one in concrete, the other in process of being so emplaced. Two additional weapons of this type were sited to fire on Tanapag Harbor, with one gun in an open emplacement 4 feet deep, and the other in a recently completed concrete casemate. East of Mutcho Point there were four of these weapons, each in circular emplacements 5 feet deep and 25 feet in diameter, and a number of single weapons also were set up at carefully chosen locations. Thirty-two of the weapons were found in storage awaiting transportation to other island bases.

On Biak a battery of the 120-mm dual-purpose guns was emplaced in pits approximately 8 feet deep and 28 feet in diameter. Six to eight ready magazines, each of 12-rounds capacity, were spaced around the pits which were reinforced with logs and oil drums. The guns were sited in an arc atop a high ridge and were well placed both for horizontal and antiaircraft fire. It is believed that they were brought to Biak in a "knocked down" form and were assembled in their pit emplacements.

Figure 57.—Two types of emplacements for the Model 10 (1921) 120-mm dual-purpose gun.

Figure 58.—Model 10 (1921) 120-mm dual-purpose gun. Note revetment details and ammunition storage.

The Model 10 is mounted on a pedestal which usually is set in concrete. A large base plate, or spade, is buried in the floor of each gun pit to provide a stable foundation. One such plate measured 28 by 30 feet and was made in sections welded together as the plate was assembled in the pit.

The gun is pointed and trained manually. Its barrel is 12 feet (45 calibers) in length. Traverse of the weapon is 360 degrees; elevation is 85 degrees and depression minus 5 degrees. Two large recoil cylinders are set side by side above the barrel. The breech is of the sliding-wedge type. The gun is equipped with a shield, three-eighths of an inch in thickness, but this is splinter proof only. Muzzle velocity is about 2,600 feet per second. The maximum horizontal range is reported at 18,000 feet, and the vertical is approximately 35,000 feet. This weapon should not be confused with the Japanese Navy Model 3 (1914) 12-cm gun which has a rotating breechblock and an elevation of only 55 degrees.

Figure 59.—Installing one gun of a twin-mount 127-mm Model 89 gun.

On Kiska the fire control unit of a battery was equipped with 3-meter height finders, 10-cm binoculars, and data computers. Batteries on Betio had range finders, sound locaters, and 90-cm and 150-cm searchlights located to illuminate both air and water targets.

The most widely used of Japanese dual-purpose guns encountered to date is the Model 88 (1928) 75-mm antiaircraft guns. Twenty-two of these weapons were emplaced on Kiska, 26 on Attu, and 8 on Betio. A four-gun battery usually is set up in the shape of an **L**. On Tarawa, the guns were emplaced in circular pits about 5 feet below ground level where the 5 spider legs of the guns rested on a concrete base. The sides of the pit were revetted by sand-filled oil drums and 1-inch boards secured by vertical coconut log piles; in some cases, coconut log walls constituted the revetment. On Betio, the inshore side of the gun position was lower than the seaward side to permit maximum depression of the weapon for effective antiboat fire.

The gun is a semiautomatic loading and firing weapon. Its over-all length is 16 feet, 6 inches, and the tube is 10 feet, 10 inches long. The rifling, which is of the uniform right hand twist pattern, extends for 101.5 inches of the tube length. There are 28 lands and grooves. The breech-block is a semiautomatic, sliding-wedge model, and the firing mechanism is of the continuous-pull percussion type.

Figure 60.—Model 88 (1928) 75-mm dual-purpose gun.

The gun can be traversed 360 degrees in 5 minutes. Its elevation is 85 degrees and the depression 0 degrees. Maximum rate of fire is 15 to 20 rounds per minute. Muzzle velocity is 2,360 feet per second, and the maximum vertical range is 29,850 feet. The gun can fire AA pointed shell, HE, shrapnel, smoke, incendiary, and illuminating shells. Usually, Model 90 AA pointed shells are fired, with a Model 89 30-second combination time fuze that gives both point-detonating and time effects. For traction two rubber-tired wheels are attached, and the limbered gun is drawn by truck or tractor.

Four Model 10 (1921) 3-inch (76.2-mm) dual-purpose guns were found on Kwajalein; this weapon also was encountered on Roi, Namur, and Eniwetok. The weapon is called a "high-angled gun" by the Japanese and is used both for antiaircraft missions and beach defense. In most cases, the guns have been set up in open emplacements which were surrounded by mounded coral and earth ramparts. In contrast to other Japanese gun positions, it has been noted that the cover and camouflage of these 3-inch gun emplacements frequently have been inadequate.

The gun, which is mounted on a pedestal, has a barrel length of 10 feet, 8½ inches. To compensate for its muzzle preponderance, an equilibrator is mounted in the pedestal. The breechblock is of the sliding-wedge type, and the recoil system is hyropneumatic. The weapon has a 360-degree traverse and a 75-degree elevation. Its muzzle velocity is reported at

Figure 61.—Model 10 (1921) 3-inch (76.2-mm) naval dual-purpose gun in banked emplacement. Note sand-filled oil drums used for revetting.

2,240 feet per second, and the maximum vertical range is about 26,000 feet. An HE projectile weighing 2.7 pounds is fired at a maximum rate of 8 to 10 rounds per minute.

Figure 62.—Model 10 (1921) 3-inch (76.2-mm) naval dual-purpose gun captured on Guadalcanal.

During the New Georgia campaign and on Kolombangara a number of Vickers type, 40-mm machine cannon were found with both single and twin mounts. It has been reported that the single-mounted guns of this type are British-made, while the dual-mount weapons are Japanese copies of the original British design.

Figure 63.—Vickers type, 40-mm machine cannon, single mount.

Both versions are recoil-operated, water-cooled, weapons fed by link belts. They can be employed for either automatic or semiautomatic fire. Both single and twin versions are mounted on pedestals, and have a 360-degree traverse, an 85-degree elevation, and a minus 5-degree depression. The cooling system consists of a circular water jacket, 50 inches long and 6 inches in diameter, with the barrel running though the lower part of the jacket. Feed is by means of metallic link belts, held in rectangular *hoppers* located on the sides of the mount. These hoppers are replaced when emptied by loaded ones.

An automatic fuze setter is installed on the twin-mount version only. The types of equilibrators constitute another significant difference between the single- and dual-mount versions of the weapon. The single-mount gun has a counter-balance weight on the right side just behind the feed hopper. The dual-mount has equilibrators of the spring-loaded cable type, one for each gun, located on the upper side of each, approximately at the center of balance. They are so adjusted as to permit rapid elevation and depression.

The guns are fired from the left side only, by means of foot-pedal triggers. The triggers of the twin-mount fire independently if desired. Five types of ammunition have been found thus far: AP with base-detonating fuze; HE with point-detonating, super-sensitive fuze (no tracer); HE time-fuzed projectile (no tracer); tracer ammunition with empty projectile; and practice shell (inert) for training purposes.

Figure 64.—Vickers type, 40-mm machine cannon, twin mount.

Much more common is the Model 98 (1938) 20-mm antiaircraft and antitank machine cannon. Ordinarily it is emplaced on its three spider legs in revetments, 4 to 5 feet deep and 8 to 10 feet in diameter, with the parapet 1 to 2 feet in height. Sides of the revetments have been very smooth in positions observed, and ammunition has been kept in dugouts in the wall of the position.

The gun has a barrel 7 feet long, and two recuperators under the tube. A horse-draft weapon, it weighs 840 pounds without the wheels. Its traverse is 360 degrees; elevation is 85 degrees and depression minus 10 degrees. Its muzzle velocity is 2,720 feet per second, and the maximum ranges are approximately 5,450 yards horizontal and 4,000 yards vertical. It normally is used to fire both AP and HE ammunition in equal proportions.

Figure 65.—Model 98 (1938) 20-mm machine cannon.

The Model 96 (1936) Type 2 25-mm antiaircraft and antitank automatic cannon is widely employed. A naval weapon, it is gas-operated, air-cooled, and magazine-fed, and can be used for either automatic or semiautomatic fire. It often is sited to defend airstrips or other major installations, and has been found on both dual- and triple-fixed mounts, usually in revetments about 15 feet in diameter. On Kiska, two of these weapons were sited near steel command posts. On Saipan, dual-mounted guns were found on steel sleds on which they were towed from one position to another.

The gun has a full 360-degree traverse, an elevation of 80 degrees, and a depression of minus 10 degrees which makes it very effective for direct-fire missions against ground targets. A single gun weighs 246 pounds; in triple mount the weight is 5,330 pounds. The muzzle velocity is 2,978 feet per second, and the estimated vertical range 14,000 feet. The magazine holds 15 shells, usually with one tracer, to every four HE.

Figure 66.—Views of 25-mm naval automatic cannon, twin mount

Figure 67.—25-mm automatic cannon, triple mount.

Mobile Guns

The heaviest Japanese mobile antiaircraft weapon is the Model 14 (1925) 105-mm antiaircraft gun which also is capable of use in dual-purpose roles. As originally designed, it was not satisfactory in view of its relatively low muzzle velocity and unwieldiness in transport. The gun has not been captured in any of the Allied campaigns to date; if used at all, it probably is installed in Japan proper in static or semistatic roles.

The gun, which weighs 11,424 pounds in firing position and 11,220 in traveling position, has six detachable outriggers. For transport, it is a trailer type with two bogies. The barrel, which is of two-piece construction consisting of a jacket and a slightly tapered liner, has an over-all length of 13 feet, 9 inches, and it is rifled with 32 lands and grooves for 11.016 feet of its length. The breech is of the horizontal sliding-wedge type, and the recoil and counterrecoil mechanism are of the hydropneumatic variable recoil type.

Figure 68.—105-mm army type mobile antiaircraft gun.

The weapon has a 360-degree traverse; maximum elevation is 85 degrees and depression is 0 degrees. Muzzle velocity is reported as 2,300 feet per second. The maximum horizontal range (unconfirmed) is 20,000 feet, while the vertical is 36,000 feet. The gun fires HE shells weighing 35.2 pounds. A combination on-and-off carriage fire control system, similar to that for the Model 88 (1928) 75-mm antiaircraft gun, presumably is employed.

Figure 69.—105-mm antiaircraft gun with crew.

Fixed Guns

The heaviest fixed dual-purpose gun found in combat theaters thus far is the twin-mount Model 89 (1929) 127-mm antiaircraft gun which is 40 calibers in length. On Betio, two-gun batteries were emplaced on two locations. Emplacements were constructed of concrete, banked with sand and coral from ground level to the brim of the concrete parapets. The guns were about 40 yards apart. At equal intervals around the parapet were 10 ammunition ready-boxes, each with 12 rounds of ammunition. The main ammunition dumps were in four bomb-proof, sand-covered concrete buildings. Quarters for gun personnel were located to the rear and outward flank of each emplacement. Fire control was exercised from a sand-covered concrete structure, 30 feet square and 15 feet above ground, protected at its corners by four 7.7-mm light machine guns. A 150-cm Model 1933 searchlight was set up on each flank of the installations.

Figure 70.—Model 89 (1929) 127-mm twin-mount naval dual-purpose gun.

Figure 71.—Views of Model 89 (1929) twin-mount naval dual-purpose gun.

Figure 72.—Twin-mount Model 89 (1929) naval dual-purpose gun.

Heavy Japanese antiaircraft guns frequently have been emplaced in batteries of three, set up in a triangular pattern with the apex toward the coast line. Two such installations were set up on Wake, and there also was one on Mili. In the South Pacific, however, the guns more commonly have been set up in a line or in an arc.

Two of these weapons were found on Kwajalein. There were four circular concrete emplacements of concrete, masonry, and earth. One was for fire control installations, while each of the the other three was designed as a gun position, two of which had the guns installed.

The gun tube is 40 calibers in length. The weapon has a traverse of 360 degrees and can be elevated to 85 degrees. Muzzle velocity is reported at 2,370 feet per second, while maximum horizontal range is believed to be about 10,000 feet, and vertical range 35,000 feet. The rate of fire is 8 to 10 rounds per minute for each barrel.

Figure 73.—Twin-mount 127-mm naval dual-purpose gun positions on Betio.

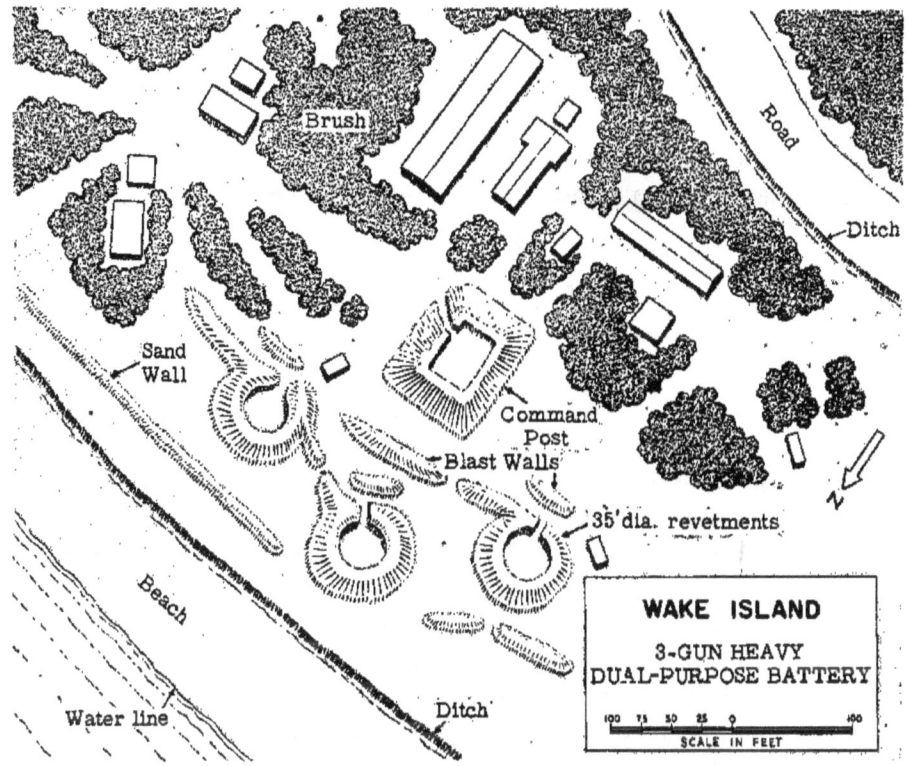

Figure 74.—Diagram of 3-gun dual-purpose battery on Wake island.

Figure 75.—Japanese 75-mm antiaircraft gun on Guam. This gun was part of a six-gun battery.

The 5-inch standard naval antiaircraft gun also may be found emplaced in coast defense positions. It is 50 calibers in length and fires a 63-pound shell which attains 1.5-inch armor penetration at 20,000 yards. Its muzzle velocity is 2,900 feet per second, and maximum range is 21,000 yards. It has a 360-degree traverse and a maximum elevation of 85 degrees.

Machine Guns

Heavy Machine Guns

A prominent part in Japanese coast defense plans has been assigned to the Model 93 (1933) 13-mm heavy machine gun. This air-cooled, gas-operated, and magazine-fed dual-purpose weapon may be encountered on both single and dual pedestal mounts. Approximately 50 calibers long, the single weapon weighs 87 pounds. It fires ball ammunition with a muzzle velocity of 2,210 feet per second, and armor piercing with a muzzle velocity of 2,280 feet per second. Estimated rate of fire is 450 rounds per minute, and maximum vertical range is approximately 13,000 feet. The two guns on the dual version are mounted separately and can be stripped from the mount individually. Each gun is cocked separately by pulling back the respective cocking handles on the sides of the receivers. Box-type magazines hold 20 rounds each, and the guns are fired by pressing on the pedals. The weapon has been encountered in coast defense installations, sited primarily to deliver frontal or flanking fire on beaches. On Betio, this weapon was installed at frequent intervals along the north and east coasts, sited to cover approaches between beach obstacles frontally and to deliver flanking fire on the reef barrier.

If the single-mount version is employed, several different types of emplacements may be utilized. The pits are about 4 feet deep, and the gun pedestal is elevated to about that same height above the floor, bringing the gun 1 to 1½ feet above the surrounding ground level. Emplacements may be hexagonal shape, with an inner diameter of about 10 feet, and the retaining walls are composed of a layer of horizontally-placed logs or boards with sandbag parapets. Square positions also have been found, measuring about 10 feet on a side. Occasionally, the single-mount gun has been found in square or hexagonal emplacements, the sides of which were lined with a wall of sand- or earth-filled bags, 2 feet thick, contained by sheet iron and posts.

The dual-mount pedestal, which measures 6 feet across its base and 4 feet in height, usually is buried in sand to the upper circular flange. The dual mount usually is sited in pear-shaped emplacements, 10 feet across at the rear and somewhat narrower in front. The positions are about 3 feet high in the rear and a foot lower in front. Walls of the emplacements are composed of sandbags 3 feet thick, banked on the outside with soft sand. Square positions also have been found, especially on top of ammunition magazines and similar installations. These have been walled by boards and banked by sand bags and loose sand to a thickness of about 3 to 4 feet.

The Model 92 (1932) 7.7-mm heavy machine gun also is widely used by the Japanese in coastal defenses. It normally is mounted on a tripod and readily can be adapted for use as an antiaircraft weapon. Two types of emplacements were used for this weapon on Betio, especially along the west and northwest coasts. The single-port type was used for frontal fire. Such positions, usually about 18 to 20 feet long, were built of coconut logs, with the sides banked with sand or coral both for protection and camouflage. The emplacements were connected by revetted communication trenches to shelters, rifle pits, command posts, and ammunition dumps, and were compartmented to protect ammunition. Double-port emplacements were used to deliver flanking fire. Most of them could mount two guns, although some possibly accommodated a 13-mm gun in addition to two of the 7.7-mm models. The double-port emplacements, from which flanking fire was delivered along the tactical wire and obstacles on the Betio beaches, could not be used for frontal fire. This fire mission was left exclusively to single-port installations. Back from the coast, 7.7-mm heavy machine guns were found in open emplacements which consisted of circular pits sunk into the ground and revetted with boards, corrugated sheet steel, and sandbags. A log or sand-filled oil drum frequently served as a pedestal upon which the guns were mounted.

The Model 92 (1932) 7.7-mm heavy machine gun is a modified Hotchkiss type. It is gas-operated, air-cooled, and full automatic only. Because of the relatively slow rate of fire (200 rounds per minute effective, 450 rounds per minute cyclic), the gun seldom overheats, and the life of the barrel therefore is unusually long. The weapon has a traverse of 360 degrees and an elevation, with tripod mount, of 11 degrees. With the tripod it weighs 122 pounds. Its maximum range is about 4,500 yards, and the effective range approximately 1,500 yards. Semirimmed ammunition in ball, tracer, or armor-piercing forms is used, and the Model 99 (1939) 7.7-mm cartridges also can be utilized if loaded in 30-round feed strips. Three telescopic sights are available for use with the Model 92, and a mount for the sight is located on the base of the receiver.

Light Machine Guns

Most light machine-gun positions also can be used interchangeably as rifle pits, in both the covered and the open forms. Along the Tarawa barricade the pits were covered by at least one layer of 10-inch coconut logs and had small ports, 12 inches by 6 inches, from which only frontal fire could be delivered. Inside measurements of the positions were approximately 4 by 4 by 4 feet, and there were small fire steps under the ports for the emplacement of the guns. A four-foot blast wall was located just behind the entrance. A number of the positions were connected at the rear by communication trenches, some of which were revetted and covered.

Open positions, on the other hand, were mere slots in the beach barricade, protected by brace-logs, sand, and board revetments. These were used only for rifles and light machine guns. Concrete light machine-gun emplacements with walls and top 14 inches thick, reinforced with ½-inch steel wire, also were sited ahead of the beach barricade. They had multiple firing ports and were used to deliver both frontal and flank fire. The positions were connected with the barricade by tunnels and communication trenches.

The most commonly used weapon was the Model 92 (1932) Lewis-type 7.7-mm light machine gun. This is a gas-operated, full-automatic weapon which uses rimless cartridges only, fed from a 30-round box magazine. The gun weighs 20 pounds without the magazine. It has an effective range of about 1,500 yards and a maximum of approximately 3,800 yards. Effective rate of fire is 250 rounds per minute.

CHAPTER VI
Detection and Communication

Radar

Present Japanese radar equipment is considered inferior to that of the Allies, but there are indications that it will be improved and that use of all types of radar can be anticipated. Although there is no concrete evidence as yet that Japanese radar has been improved in performance, there are indications that the newer types are of higher power output, have lower pulse widths, and, in general, are more advanced in design than the equipment captured up to the present time.

Radar search receivers are extensively employed. They would provide excellent warning of the approach of Allied aircraft or surface vessels, and it is considered probable that they are so employed in areas where Japanese radar coverage is inadequate. The Japanese appear to be extremely conscious of the fact that their radar transmissions can be intercepted. Aircraft in the Southwest Pacific have noted that on numerous occasions the Japanese take their radar off the air when the site is approached. Apparently they fear the possibility of Allied aircraft homing on their radars.

The Japanese apparently are setting up a new system of radar designation. Formerly, installations were referred to by mark, model, modification, and type. According to the new system of designation, only a mark number is given.

Description of Early Warning Equipment

The first known type of Japanese radar, probably in use as an early warning air search radar since January 1942, is the Mark II, sometimes referred to as Mark I, Model 1, Type 2. This model has been found at Guadalcanal, Kiska, Roi, Kwajalein, and Saipan, and, although newer installations may use a modification of this model, the Mark II undoubtedly still is extensively used by the Japanese.

The equipment is housed in a wooden shack with 140 by 29 feet antenna array attached to one side. It usually is mounted on a concrete base and rotates through 360 degrees, either by manual control or by automatic, motor-driven sweep. The transmitter is a push-pull oscillator using a copper "can" cavity resonator, followed by a neutralized push-pull, balanced, tuned-line amplifier. The frequency range is approximately 90 to 105 megacycles, but operation is recommended below 100 megacycles for better efficiency. The rated peak power output is 3 kilowatts.

The equipment is poor for surface search. The antenna beam width is 25 degrees, and bearing accuracy within 5 degrees, but there is little low-angle radiation. The indicator range accuracy on "A" type presentation is about 500 yards. The average range to the first detection of aircraft is about 32 nautical miles; to surface craft about 10 miles, with minimum range limit of about 2 miles.

So far, two modifications of the Mark II have been reported. Modification 1, a somewhat improved version with similar performance and employing the same mattress-like antenna, was developed in August 1942, and examples of this equipment have been captured at Attu, Makin, and Tarawa. According to Japanese documents, Modification 2 of Mark I, Model 1, soon will replace the earlier radars, which it resembles in general appearance. The new range limit, however, is 164 nautical miles—twice the rated range of Modification 1.

Two radar installations on Makin were mounted in the same way as the two on Tarawa. An octagonal reinforced concrete base, 10 feet in diameter, supported a steel turntable, 7 feet in diameter. On the turntable were 4 steel beams, each 15 feet long, upon which was built the 10-foot square prefabricated wooden shack. A large, cage-like antenna structure was supported in a vertical position across the ends of the steel beams. The steel antenna framework was 14 feet high, 18 feet wide, and 28 inches deep. A horizontal partition extended across the middle of the frame. Frame and partition were covered on all sides with number 8 galvanized iron wire in a 1½-inch mesh.

A radar installation found on Peleliu was located in the center of a revetment, 4 feet high, surrounded by coconut trees. Several searchlights and 4.7-inch guns were emplaced in the vicinity. The radar equipment was mounted on a concrete base at ground level. The mount revolved on the base, and the pointer, trainer, and two operators rode the mount on the seats with which it was provided.

Three antenna bays, mounted on a 25¾-foot horizontal beam, were on top of the large frame which supported the entire unit. All antenna elements were lengths of half-inch copper tubing mounted by ceramic insulators to wooden frames.

The radar, which had a frequency of 203 megacycles, a pulse repetition frequency of about 2000 cycles, and a pulse duration of 3 microseconds, delivered a peak power of 30 kilowatts.

Another fixed installation aircraft warning radar is the Mark III. Very little is known about this equipment. It is thought to be primarily an army radar for early warning of approaching aircraft. The transmitter

Figure 76.—Japanese radar screen.

is believed to be geographically separated from the receiving station—or stations. Operation presumably is based on the Doppler effect—to detect aircraft presence and range only. It is said to give effective air warning at a maximum range of 100 miles and to have a power output of 500 watts. Recent reports indicate that the Japanese have ceased manufacturing this model.

The Mark 12, formerly referred to as the Mark I, Model 2 Type 2, is a mobile aircraft warning radar installation. It is mounted on a 3-ton Model 94 army trailer which can be towed by a tractor or automobile, but it must work in conjunction with a separate power van.

The antenna is mounted on the side of a metal cab set on a rubber-tired trailer. The antenna and cab, either manually or automatically controlled, rotate together through 360 degrees. The antenna characteristics are similar to the Mark 1 Model 1. The rated range to aircraft is 50 miles, but reported results are much less. Considerably damaged specimens of this radar have been captured on Namur and Dyaul Islands.

The Mark 13 (Mark I Model 3 Type 3) is a lightweight, easily transported radar that can be carried in aircraft or small boats and requires only 2½ hours to set up on land. This type of radar, considerably damaged, was found on Namur Island. Its rated range is 434 miles to aircraft; the accuracy ±100 m, ±10 degrees.

Another portable radar installation, about which only documentary information is available, is the Mark VI, Special Model Type 3 Air. This installation is referred to as a shore-based early warning type radar. Its rated range to aircraft detection is 21 nautical miles. It is doubtful, however, that this radar has widespread use. It probably filled the gap as a portable radar for shore use because of its light weight and small size until it was replaced by the Mark I Model 3.

Searchlight Control

The Mark 41, or Mark IV Model 3 (L), S1, is primarily a searchlight control apparatus. It was developed from captured British equipment. The receiving antenna array is attached directly to the front of the searchlight; the transmitting antenna and the pointer's scope are mounted on the searchlight controller. The effective range is quite limited—for search about 20 miles, and for tracking, about 10 miles. The ranging accuracy is ±100 meters; bearing and elevation accuracy ±1 degree for targets at about 15 degrees elevation. Error increases considerably for lower angles. Built into the equipment is a selector, or target discriminator, which enables the operator to track one plane out of a group. Part of this equipment was found on Saipan.

Radio

The principal methods of communication between Japanese units are by telephone and radio; it is a guiding principle, however, that wire is to be used whenever possible. It is presumed that this order of preference was initiated for reasons of security, rather than because of weakness in the Japanese radio organization. Wire is laid as soon as possible by the Japanese forward elements. However, when communications must be established rapidly, radio is used. After wire communications have been established, radio assumes a secondary role as a stand-by.

In Southwest Pacific operations, the Japanese use high-powered radio installations for communication from island to island. The sets used are both high and low frequency. Moreover, there is a general trend to use radio in smaller units much more at present than in the past.

The excellent camouflage and concealment of Japanese radio installations are noteworthy. Locations are carefully selected, and fullest advantage is taken of natural cover. Large antennas are arranged with ropes and pulleys so they can be raised to the tops of trees for maximum efficiency and lowered when necessary for concealment or adjustment.

A radio station is operated by a radio platoon comprised of one officer and 72 men. The platoon is divided into eight sections of nine men each. The first six sections operate Model 94 Type 4 or 2B radios with ranges up to about 15 miles. The seventh and eighth sections each operate a portable radio for air-ground liaison. Long distance radio stations are operated by a fixed radio unit with a strength of about 25 officers and men.

A great deal of the apparatus captured so far shows obsolescent design. The circuits and components are comparable with those that were in use by the Allied Nations around 1935 to 1937. Almost invariably, the transmitters and receivers have plug-in coils to cover the various bands. The power transmitters, up to 50 watts, use simple Hartley oscillator circuits, connected directly to the antenna. The smaller receivers use regenerative detectors without radio frequency amplification. While arrangements such as these are simple to service and maintain, the frequency stability suffers greatly. It would be very difficult to "net" these radio sets and keep them on frequency.

A great variety of small transceivers and transmitter-receiver combinations of one to two watts power are in use. These sets are usually man-packed. The transceivers are contained in one case, carried on the chest, while the batteries are in another case carried on the back. In transporting the small transmitter-receiver sets, the transmitter, receiver and batteries, and the hand generator for transmitter power are all carried in separate cases, making it necessary to use from two to three men to pack and operate a set.

Sets of from 10 to 50 watt power are usually of the portable type, the total apparatus being carried in four or five separate cases, and power connections being made by plugs and cables. The sets, in general, have a complexity of controls that does not lend itself to ease of operation. As an example, the Japanese Direction Finder and Intercept Finder, Model 94 Type 1, has so many controls that a comparatively long period of time must be taken to get an accurate "fix" on a transmitter.

The wide frequency range of the Japanese radio transmitters makes them capable of utilizing the frequencies most effective for sky-wave transmission at any given time. All radio transmitters so far examined, except "walkie-talkie", had one crystal furnished in addition to a master oscillator. These crystals are reported to be of excellent quality. Many ammeters both for antenna and power are supplied with separate shunts so that the same meter movement can be used with many different sets. In contrast, a multiplicity of types of radio tubes is used, complicating the supply problem. Receiving tubes are often microphonic, due to faulty construction. The supply of dry batteries is facilitated by the restriction to a very few types and battery boxes are adapted to accommodate standard types.

In spite of the facts that Japanese signal equipment is designed for maximum portability and its use in the jungle and for amphibious operations was to be expected, no attempt was made to make these sets moisture or fungus-proof. Poor grade insulating materials were used which are subject to failure under jungle conditions.

The deficiencies in radio equipment are partially offset by having well-trained operators who are capable of making good use of their equipment and give it excellent care.

Japanese radio installations on Makin Atoll were located on Butaritari Island, and since most of the equipment was manufactured in 1943, they probably constitute a representative sample of equipment utilized in shore-defense installations.

There were two radio systems, one for long range radio-telephone and radio-telegraph communication, and the other for local communication. The long-range equipment was housed in separate transmitter and receiver buildings. The former structure, a frame building 90 feet long and 31 feet wide, was heavily revetted and had compartments for transmitters, batteries, tube spare parts, and personnel. The transmitter room contained 6 transmitters, all situated along the outside walls with short antenna leads. The power distribution panel was set up on an inside wall. Outside the building were three 75-foot masts for the antenna which were of the horizontal cage type for the long-range sets and single vertical wires for the local transmitters. Transmitter equipment comprised one 1,000-watt long-wave transmitter, two 1,000-watt short-wave sets, two 500-watt short-wave sets, and one short-wave set of 100-watt capacity.

The receiving building, 78 by 33 feet, had compartments for receiving, monitoring, batteries, storage, and personnel. There were eight receivers in the receiving room, and one was installed in the monitoring compartment. There was one frequency meter, and an antenna bus to the rear of the receivers, with the antenna supported by two 60-foot masts. The receivers were 7-tube superheterodyne, battery operated, with frequency range from 20 kilocycles to 20 megacycles.

Local radio communication was centered in 7 stations, each equipped with a 100-watt semiportable AC transmitter and a 7-tube plug-in type superheterodyne receiver. Each station had an emergency gasoline-powered generator for use in the event of power failure.

Searchlights

A number of different types of searchlights, ranging in size from 60-cm diameter to 150-cm, have been found in various Japanese coast defense installations encountered to date. Two 60-cm lights were set up at Munda in circular emplacements, 8 feet in diameter and 3 to 4 feet deep. Low sod parapets, 2 to 3 feet in height, surrounded the pits with a narrow opening for an entrance. A rope net covered the light as camouflage.

A 90-cm searchlight was mounted on a command post on Tarawa to furnish illumination for a four-gun battery of 75-mm dual purpose guns which were emplaced to protect the command post.

On Kiska, two 98-cm lights were found behind the main Japanese camp, one on a fixed mount set on a concrete base within a low, built-up emplacement, 16 feet in diameter. This light was part of the installation of a battery of 75-mm anti-aircraft guns and also served to illuminate the harbor. A power sub-station stepped up the amperage from the main power station. The other 98-cm light was mounted on Little Kiska in a well-camouflaged and revetted truck, near a four-gun battery of 13-mm dual-purpose heavy machine guns. Power was supplied from a built-in generator operated by the truck motor.

One-hundred-centimeter lights were found at Vila, Munda, and Tarawa. Two on Vila were mounted in a truck park on a mobile mount. The one on Betio also was on a mobile mount in a circular excavated emplacement, 8 to 10 feet in diameter, with power furnished from a built-in generator. This light apparently served as a signal light for ships. One 100-cm searchlight also was found on Tarawa, in a circular excavated emplacement just inland from the beach, apparently located to spot hostile landing craft.

The 150-cm light also has been found in considerable numbers in defensive installations attacked by U. S. forces to date. Eight of them were found on Tarawa, with 5 on fixed mounts on 10- by 12-inch rectangular concrete structures which housed their generators. The other three were on circular concrete structures, 10 to 12 feet in diameter and 8 to 10 feet high, which, like the rectangular buildings, also housed generators.

Figure 77.—Japanese mobile searchlight.

Figure 78.—Japanese searchlight on Betio.

Two 150-cm lights were found on Kiska, one on each side of a 4.7-inch coast defense battery. They were employed primarily to illuminate night attacks, but also were available for antiaircraft defense in conjunction with a battery of 75-mm antiaircraft guns. They were housed in low, circular, built-up revetments which had a diameter of about 16 feet. Power was furnished from the main line through a sub-station equipped with 2 generators and 6 transformers. On Munda, a 150-cm light was found near a doughnut-shaped emplacement which had 42 and 45 feet outside diameters and 10 and 12 feet inside. These emplacements were made of sand, earth, and crushed coral rock. The outer revetment was higher than the inner one, and there was a shallow ditch between inner and outer revetments for passage by the operators of the lights when manually traversing the lights. There were hideouts for the lights near by, consisting of coconut-log revetted pits 9 by 10 by 7 feet, banked with earth and sand. There also were similar positions for the generators.

Figure 79.—Searchlight captured near Munda airfield.

At Vila one 150-cm light was found in a circular emplacement 20 feet in diameter, while another was set up in a circle made of earth-filled oil drums, 16 feet in diameter. The generator was installed in a similar emplacement in a nearby grove. On Wake, three of these lights have been identified on roofs of circular concrete structures, 10 to 12 feet in diameter; two of them furnished illumination for coast defense batteries. On Mili Island, two 150-cm lights flanked a three-gun heavy coast defense battery. They are installed on circular platforms, 10 feet in diameter, mounted on high, circular, earth revetments. Installations of the 150-cm light also have been observed on Maleolap, Paramushiru, and at Rabaul.

Performance data on Japanese searchlights thus far is virtually nonexistent. The Japanese state, however, that the following figures apply to the 90-cm light, presumably the Model 96 (1936).

Source of power	100 volts D. C.
Arc voltage	85 volts
Arc current	200 amperes
Length of arc	1.17 inches
Positive carbon:	
Diameter	.468 inch
Length	27.3 inches
Combustion period	30 minutes (approx.)
Negative carbon:	
Diameter	.468 inch
Length	27.3 inches
Combustion period	60 minutes (approx.)
Reflector:	
Type	navy, parabolic
Effective diameter	35.1 inches
Focal distance	14.586 inches
Glass front:	
Type	flat
Effective diameter	35.1 inches
Traverse	180 degrees, right; 180 degrees, left
Elevation	90 degrees
Depression	20 degrees (minus)

This light, used primarily for the illumination of airfields, normally is mounted on a truck.

Figure 80.—Searchlight and sound detector.

www.ingramcontent.com/pod-product-compliance
Lightning Source LLC
Chambersburg PA
CBHW080516110426
42742CB00017B/3134